FROM ZERO TO HERO

HOW TO MAKE MONEY IN YOUR FIRST YEAR OF NETWORK MARKETING WITH A PROVEN 8 STEP SYSTEM

INFINITY MASTERY SERIES BOOK 1

www.JustAskChristopher.com

Limits Of Liability & Disclaimer Of Warranty

Warning and disclaimer

Contents

Who Is Christopher Peacock?

Hi my name is Christopher Peacock, I've been a Coach and Trainer since early 2000, I started my first Business in the beginning of 2004 and I was introduced to Network Marketing in 2007; it took me eight years before I found the right company and got started. Now those of you already in the industry will be smiling right now as you, like me now, know that in eight years you can build a hugely successful Network Marketing Business! In fact you can easily create your financial freedom in that time frame! Well, such is my experience, however when I finally got started I never looked back!

I did so with an Organic Super-food company. Many people had tried to recruit me into their Health and Wellness company before but working as a high level Health Professional I wouldn't choose just any product line to promote, they had to be of the highest standards and all the companies I was presented with just didn't cut it. This was the beginning of my journey into Network Marketing!

I worked solid with this company for about 3 years and achieved mediocre success. I was mentored during this time for 2 years by the

Top Networker in Canada, who was personally mentored by Dexter Jager for 10 years. I took on some additional companies thinking I could work two companies or more at the same time - I couldn't! When I thought I was on to a winner with a Bitcoin platform, I ended up getting scammed.

During this time I had many lessons not only in how to build the business but also on a personal level about myself. I learned that consumer based products and consumerism just wasn't and isn't for me. What I became drawn to and much more interested in was and is Wealth Creation; Assets. Products that grow in Value the longer you hold on to them vs lotions potions powders and pills you consume and ingest. Now don't get me wrong, there's nothing wrong with companies that have consumable products, for me those business models didn't work out.

My success came with Wealth Creation and Assets. I partnered with a company in the beginning of 2018 and I've never looked back having achieved huge success!

> ➢ in my 1st month my commissions paid for the initial cost to setup my business
>
> ➢ by 4 months I was recognised for my achievements with my very own special wall plague positioned up in the Head Office
>
> ➢ by 12 months I replaced and increased my full time income.
>
> ➢ by 20 months I hit the top rank in the company's compensation plan.

- ➢ by 2 years I increased my income by 10x
- ➢ during this time I'd hit a number of incentive gifts offered by the company
- ➢ I'd built a number of leaders within my team

And the company was and is on a massive growth phase too! So welcome to the first in the Infinity Mastery series of books - dive in, and I hope you enjoy it!

Chapter 1 – Vision

Welcome to "From Zero To Hero - How To Make Money In Your First Year Of Network Marketing With A Proven 8 Step System." This book was originally created by a series of live interviews – that's why it reads like a conversation rather than as a traditional book that talks "at you." I want you to feel that I am talking "with you", much like a close friend or relative. I felt that creating the material this way would make it easier for you to grasp the topics and put them to use quickly, rather than wading through hundreds of pages.

So relax, grab a pen and paper and get ready to take your financial future to the next level. Let's get started with the importance of having a vision...

JC:

Why is it important to have a vision?

CP:

The benefit of having a vision is to give you direction, so you have an idea of where you're heading. One of the steps I've found helpful in the businesses that I've had previously, in the industries that I've worked on, is knowing where I wanted to go. When I was younger, I always aspired to have a five-year goal or a 10-year goal. When it was a specific goal I was heading to, I'd know why I was taking action. I had a purpose; I had direction. Having a vision is a bit like having a GPS – it keeps you going forward towards your goal or aspiration.

JC:

So, if you don't have that kind of vision in place, there's no launching pad?

CP:

If you've not got visions in place, your motivation and your persistence vary; you can lose track of why you are doing this. If you hit obstacles or challenges, it's going to be much easier to fall off the bandwagon. For example, a lot of people start a home-based business and for the first time, they've not started with any training, or any coaching or support. Although that support is available, sometimes it's limited. So if you don't have a vision, I just think that you tend to lose your way. A vision keeps you focused. It keeps you moving forward.

It reminds me of golf – when you fall off the beaten path and you're in the rough looking for your golf ball. It reminds you of where you're supposed to be going.

No matter who you listen to or read, whoever gurus you aspire to, whatever you want to model, they all talk about it. Tony Robbins, Bob

Proctor, they all speak about it... the law of attraction and creating dream boards or vision boards. It's about keeping yourself inspired and motivated.

It's a way to be self-motivated to be self-reliant. When we're coming from an employed – or employee – mindset, we're usually handheld through what we're supposed to do. We show up and do the jobs that were given. In our education system we were also dictated in how and what we learned. We're not educated to be thinkers; we're educated to be followers.

This sort of dictation makes it very difficult for anyone to be self-reliant, because for many, many years, they've been told what to do. Whereas now, in your business, you're on your own. You need to have a number of tools in place to keep you on the right path and to stop yourself from wandering off it. I strongly believe that vision boards and the processes that we will discuss in this book, will help you keep on the straight and narrow. A vision reminds you that it's not just about the money – it's about the lifestyle, it's about what you want to provide for your family. It's that next level up, so it's keeping you focused.

JC:

When you get off track, you struggle?

CP:

Yes. When you get off track, your vision will bring you back. It's like I said before, you could literally use it as an exercise to focus your intention and have it in your in your mindset. The more you think about it, the more it can manifest. Connect this to the law of attraction theory, where your attention and energy goes, the energy flows, which I think is the Napoleon Hill quote, I think.

Without a vision, how long are you likely to be dedicated to what it is you're trying to achieve? It's a bit like the gold at the end of your path. The vision is your yellow brick road to your treasures.

JC:

I know what you're saying. Every top performer has that vision in their head, every football team goes out on that pitch with a win in their head. Visualisation fires the same neural pathways and therefore, statistically, mental rehearsal improves your chances of achieving your goal. How do you set out your vision?

CP:

Breaking down the vision makes it more segmented and easier to conceptualise. I like to break it down into 5 categories, and it's the way my mentor broke it down to me. The first element is, who are you? In your mind's eye and the vision that you have of yourself, when you are successful, or when you've achieved whatever it is that you want to achieve, who are you? How do you look? How do you feel? What's your posture like? How's your physical health? How's your mental health? What is your style and fashion? How do you look? How are you perceived? So, the first one is, who are you? For me personally, it's who am I when I'm successful. Your label may not be about success – it may be something else. But for me, it is about success.

The second one is, what's the setting for your dream lifestyle? What's your backdrop? What's your background? What's the setting? Are you somewhere exotic and tropical? Are you in nature, by the lakeside? Do you have a beach lifestyle, or is your backdrop the Swiss Alps? Is it snowing, with wooden cabins, it's the scenery? So, what's your setting?

The third vision is, what is it that you want to experience? Do you want to travel? Where do you want to travel to? Are you surrounded by lots of groups of people? Are you surrounded by a close knit group of people? Think about relationships, love relationships, friend relationships, family relationships, winter holidays, exotic summer holidays, cruises, etc.

What experiences do you want to have? Do you want to be one of the first people to go up on Virgin Galactic? To be involved with the first commercial space travel?

The fourth is the toys, or all your materialistic items – the houses, the cars, the yachts, the jewellery, the clothing. You can also go into more detail. If you're talking about houses or property, for example, what does each room look like? One of the traits that has been stressed to me when it comes to vision and where most people fall down on, is that you must put in lots of detail. The more detailed, the more specific, the better. It also comes into some of the goal setting that we'll get to later on.

The fifth category is about giving. Who are you going to give back to? These could be causes, charities or non-profits, for example. Have a think about what causes are close to your heart. Is it animals? Is it children? International development and aid? Education? To whom will you give back? If you don't have the money, you can always give time to your chosen causes. But, once you build a certain level of financial stability and freedom, then you can start to bring in the financial side of giving back.

Those are the five ways I like to break down the vision. And remember as well that with each of these, you can use vision boards as visualisation exercises. These involve focusing on your visions and just daring to dream a little bit. In terms of schooling, we've almost been shut down on the ability to dream, the ability to imagine and the ability to be creative. If you were a daydreamer in school, like me, you were told off for daydreaming and for looking out the window. We were corrected when we were dreaming. And as we grew up, we dreamed a little bit less, our imagination dulled a little bit more.

One of the big changes that I've seen and felt it is when you do get back into this visualisation, this dreaming element, it starts to just pop things in your brain. It starts to open up possibility. When we were kids, we played Dungeons and Dragons, Hero Quest or World of Warcraft, games like these. All that dreaming and imagination that we did as kids got shut down, but we can reintroduce it. We can work that part of the brain. It creates inspiration, it creates motivation, it allows you to believe that something bigger than you is possible, and that you are able to achieve it. Those exercises, doing vision boards – these physical tools can expand your reality and the possibilities.

JC:

So, you're using your brain more effectively, which means you end up taking better actions or more consistent actions, which therefore means your end results are better?

CP:

Yeah. I believe it also helps you become more positive in life. You look on life more positively rather than negatively. I think we all need to do a bit more positive thinking in all areas of life. Being more positive naturally creates more positivity and possibility in our lives. It also creates metaphysical shifts. It shifts chemical reactions within the body and what you are projecting out into the world. If you're being more positive, you're also more attractive to other people. This pays off in a relationship industry where you build connections and relationships with people. People work with people. It doesn't necessary matter what the product or the company is – it's more to do with, who are you? Do I really want to work with you? Are you a nice person? If you're a positive person who has a positive outlook on life, who is a dreamer, who aspires for more and aspires for bigger and believes it's possible, that's inspiring. So this simple little visualisation exercise, which is just the beginning, has a ripple effect that shouldn't be underestimated.

JC:

So how does someone think about creating that vision?

CP:

I simply just went on Google and found a bunch of images, pulled the images off Google Images and put them into a PowerPoint. I made a collage of lots of different images, and then just printed off as A4 or A3. I've got bigger ones now, but this depends on how much space you've got and how many vision boards. Five A3 posters takes up a lot of space. That's the simplest way of doing it. You need to have these vision boards and put them somewhere you'll always see them. I've got them sitting in my office - right now they're around my screen, and every day that I'm working from this space that I'm looking at them, my subconscious can see in my peripheral vision. They've been here for a number of years, since I've done this sort of training and mentoring.

The traditional method is to get magazines and scrapbooks. Get out the pens, the sticky tape, the pritt stick, and make it that way. Get a big bit of paper and then cut things out and stick them on. You can make it more of an exercise. It can be fun; you can do it with family and make it a fun bonding exercise.

Use the five categories and find images to represent your ideas. What do you want? How do you see yourself? What's the backdrop for your dream life? What are the experiences you want to have? What toys do you want? What causes do you want to give back to?

Keep it simple – go with your gut instinct. The more you consciously try, the more you complicate it in your mind and you'll never get started. So what do you like? Well, I like exotic holidays. Type in 'exotic holidays' search Google Images and just look for things that you like. If you are more introverted, you might want a wooden cabin in the Swiss Alps. Whatever it is, let yourself dream.

JC:

And we both know that then what starts to happen, you start to notice your Reticular Activation System. Someone said to me, have you seen the new Chrysler Crossfire? Wait till you see it, it has this gorgeous square exhaust at the back. Then, a couple days later I was in Glasgow, and I saw this car sitting in front of me with an interesting pair of exhaust. It was the Chrysler Crossfire. From then on, I couldn't not see them. They were everywhere, and that wasn't even one of my goals – a client of mine was talking about it. That's the way it works. All of a sudden, your radar switches on you start seeing things – the coincidences increase.

CP:

That's why you need to always have the vision boards around. Make a point of setting time to do the daily visualization as it activates that part of your brain.

JC:

Yeah, repetition is key. The unconscious mind is impressed by repetition and colour and the right brain, etc. So, if you are going to challenge your reader to take a next step, I imagine that would be to write down these five different categories and write down the answers to those questions?

CP:

Yeah, start with a writing exercise so you've got something to work from. For those who struggle with dreaming, this is especially useful. To begin with, I never dreamed, and my imagination's terrible. So, write stuff down to have a starting point.

Afterwards, put the answers into picture form.

Along with the vision boards, you want to be setting your goals as well. The goals are part of the vision – the vision is how it all works. But what is it that you want to achieve, specifically? You've got to have your short term, medium term and long-term goals. It's best to start small; it doesn't need to be massive goals like the 10-bedroom house of the Bugatti supercar. When I started my business, my short-term goal was to get the capital back that it cost me to start the business. Maybe that will be a two-week goal or a four-week goal. Alternatively, maybe I want to enrol 5 to 10 people in my first week. The goal setting and measuring is important.

That also comes into the first step of the vision because you've got your dream, you've got your vision, and now you need to set some goals of how you're going to move forward. Using short term, medium term, and long term is a good way to do it.

JC:

What timescales will you put to that?

CP:

It's quite individual. Like I said, short term, medium term, long term. Your short term could be within your first week or your first month, your medium could be four to six months, and long term could be 12 months later. A year is still small for me, but for someone who's getting started, I think the closer the better.

Doing 6 to 12 months, 5 years or even going as far as 10 years, I think are too big. People need to keep their attention spans activated. We need the instant gratification that we get nowadays with the speed of technology and the speed of the internet increasing. We are able to get everything with a click. We get any type of food delivered to us. We get access to everything.

A common piece of advice is to keep your goals smart. The S-M-A-R-T, and I like to throw in the R at the end. So SMARTR, which we break it all down, you get your Specific, Measurable, Attainable, Realistic, Time frame. Then, a lot of people miss out on Reward.

When you've achieved your goal, do you reward yourself? If you come in first in a race or a competition, you get rewards – you get the gold medal or the silver medal. But in life, we forget to reward ourselves. There's a big impact on the subconscious, on a vibrational level energetic level, on our mind set, when we reward ourselves for hitting our goals. Many people are quite happy to go out, work hard and achieve the goal. Then onto the next goal. By doing this, you're teaching your subconscious that you'll always working and that there's no reward. So, why would you continue? However, if you bring in the reward at the end of every goal – no matter how small or how large – you're teaching your subconscious that there's a reason for I'm working hard. Maybe you've committed to a certain level and you've given up other things to do this and you've rescheduled my time availability, you've rescheduled commitments, and you're going to put energy, focus and dedication into this business. Why? Because you're going to reward yourself regularly.

My day job doesn't reward me. I get a pay check, but I exchange time for money, and I might get a 1% pay rise at the end of the year, if you're lucky. That's not a huge reward. Teaching our subconscious that we reward ourselves when we hit our achievements, when we hit our goals, will enable you to achieve them more quickly. It's a signal going out to the universe on a vibrational, energetic level.

JC

It's how you train a dolphin to jump over the rope, you know? You have to treat yourself, condition yourself with rewards, so you keep performing. If you put together your vision, good things happen.

CP:

I think you've got to question, why am I doing this? Once you've followed these steps, it'll all be much clearer.

Outside of the goal setting, you also need to make sure that you're tracking yourself. You've planned it and you're tracking. Make sure that it's not all just stored in your head – have it physically written down. There're a number of templates available online and these are CRM – customer relationship management – systems. When you come into this industry, I'm sure your sponsor will have some sort of tracking system that you can use and we're going to go into some others in the later chapters as well.

Chapter 2 – Committing To Your Goals

JC:

So, we're talking about commitment to your goals and sticking at it.

CP:

If you're going to create anything, you need to commit to yourself. Set some limits or some goals, and then commit to attaining them. What are you going to do, and what are you willing to commit to? A lot of people come into the network industry as a secondary job – sometimes they call it the side hustle. It's an additional or supplementary income.

The majority of people have full time employment or another primary income source. So, it's about connecting with your new venture, and allocating a certain amount of time. How much time are you willing to commit? What are you willing to do to your schedule? What commitment within your schedule will you need to build your business? Is it going to be thirty minutes a day? Is it going to be an hour a day? Is it going to be more? When is it going to be? One of the biggest issues that I've seen with people is a lack of consistency.

Having a firm commitment, committing to yourself and committing to your business avoids that lack of consistency. On a daily basis, how many people will you speak to? How long will you spend?

What study materials are you going to use for your business? What are you listening to and reading? Are you getting coached? If so, what's your coaching schedule?

You'll start well but, as we all know, it's easy to fall off the wagon. Especially around New Year, many people commit to a new healthy lifestyle, but it lasts for a weekend or week at the most. If we use that analogy for business, and especially when people are starting something completely new, it's very easy to fall off the wagon. It's easy to become demotivated or to lose consistency moving forward. So, the commitment element is about deciding what you're going to attain and sticking to the plan. It's also about how involved you are within your business community. What is your relationship to the person that introduced you to this business? What community support structure is available? Is it a Facebook group or another social media group? Is it a local group where you host or where you're part of a hosted event? Is it for training purposes or for promotional purposes? The other commitment is what's known as product loyalty. Your business has products that need promoting – how loyal are you to your products?

Basically, if you are committed to your business. You should be utilising the services or products that you're offering, whether that's consumer based, asset based, wealth creation based, service based or some form of a provision. You should be actively involved. If you get a backup order or a monthly repeating purchase order of some sort, that's something you need to be plugged into and participating in. You're committed to your product. A big part of that is also if you're not doing it, why should someone else do it? Why should you look or expect someone to do a backup order, do a monthly order, if you're not doing it yourself?

It you want to make a change, it's like joining the gym and paying a monthly membership. Even if you don't show up, the lights were on and the machines were on. We were here. You didn't show up. The trainers don't expect your waistline to get smaller because you're not doing the work.

If we're talking about the logical side of it... you make a commitment of an hour and you've scheduled it. If you focus on the metaphysical, spiritual or energetic side, you're making a commitment to achieve a goal to achieve a result. If you break that commitment, who did you break the commitment to? It wasn't made with anyone else - only yourself. If you're breaking a commitment or a contract to yourself, what's that teaching your subconscious? What energy or vibration are you putting out to the universe?

We spoke in the last chapter about smart goals. We had the usual SMART that everyone's heard of, and we also added that R the end, which is Reward. In the last chapter we also spoke about the power of rewarding yourself and teaching your subconscious that effort does X and receives Y.

The second step here is about your commitment. If you break your commitment to yourself, you're teaching your subconscious how easy it is. The more commitments you break with yourself, the easier it becomes to break them. You can go deep into this, or you can stay at the surface level and simply decide to commit. Decide, 'I'm going to commit to my business. I'm going to do the steps that need to be done and I'm going to do X, Y Z.'

Be clear with yourself. There is no 'hope' and there is no 'try'. In business, there is simply, 'Do' or 'Not Do'.

For example, you either call someone or you don't. There's no trying. I'm deleting 'try' from my vocabulary because it doesn't exist. You cannot try to drink water and you cannot try to build a business. You either do or you don't. There's an action involved.

JC:

You're right. I used to teach people to do hypnosis and at the end of the seminars I'd say, 'if you don't subsequently use these skills, after spending three days with your unconscious mind talking openly and freely for the first time in your life – if you suddenly shut the door and put it back in the box, what message does that impart?

If you say you're going to do something, do it. But as much as we love the end goal of the lifestyle, it will take effort to get there.

People resist the effort – its human nature. People like convenience; they like quick, easy shortcuts. They want the magic bullet and the secret formula.

There are guidelines and formulas you can follow. There's no need to reinvent the wheel. However, there's still graft, and you still have to show up. You have to show up at the gym at the right time having had the right diet and enough sleep. And you must pay your gym bill.

CP:

That's the same with the networking models. Sometimes, the dream is promoted more than the reality: the dream of financial freedom. This is where the networking models went down, or at least lost brownie points, with how people viewed it. It was all about the glory, without the reality of how much effort is needed or the highs and the lows.

All the big coaches out there – Bob Proctor, Robert Kiyosaki , Tony Robbins – all talk about having huge dreams and thinking big. Make it so big that it's uncomfortable.

If you want those big dreams and goals, and if you actually want to achieve them, it's going to take time and it's not going to be easy. That's the reality of it. It's not like magic; snap your fingers and it's there. I think the industry averages state that it'll take seven years before you're successful. Most small start-ups are self-employed people that gave up before the end of the first year.

JC:

19% of businesses survive the first five years.

CP:

Yeah. It's almost as if the numbers are against you. To firm up the commitment part, make it a realistic commitment. For example, if you're working 40 hours, don't commit to an extra 40 hours on the business. You've already got responsibilities – your family, your home, travel, etc. Some business people talk about getting five hours' sleep, starting work at 4 AM or 5 AM. Not all of us are morning people and it's important to get enough rest. We all have one thing in common – we only have 24 hours per day, so it's about what we do with those 24 hours.

So, if you're sleeping eight hours a day, then you spend an hour eating. Let's also put an hour travel aside. So that's 10 hours including travel. If you listen to Gary Vee and some other leaders online, they cut their sleep down to six hours, five hours. The point is to analyse how you're spending your time. Then, manage your time, structure your time, and then commit to it.

But, change is difficult.

This is why I said, you need to make realistic commitments and realistic adjustments to your schedule. If you don't, your commitments will be harder to maintain. By being more realistic, you'll be able to achieve, which will make you feel better and you'll continue.

It's a perpetual cycle. As you feel good about what you're doing, you'll see the results; you're getting things done and you're not hard on yourself.

If you're on public transport, audiobooks are a great way to learn. It's a good use of time when traveling as a passenger. That's two hours a day where you can be listening, you can be reading, you can be viewing YouTube videos. Or you could use that time to be contacting people. We'll talk about the contact message in the future chapters.

So, be committed to making your commitments simple, making it achievable, and then building it up based around the time that you have available.

I think everybody who's serious about making a concrete change in their reality has to understand that it's going to require effort and discipline. The fuel for that effort is your needs. The fuel for the issue is the why, and holding that picture in your head of how life will be when you get there.

JC:

So, why is it so difficult? Why do people get overwhelmed and explode? And why do leaders suddenly disappear? They start not showing up or they stop going to event: they stopped taking the product. What's going on there?

CP:

Good question.

There's any number of things that could be going on there, but it all comes back to personal development. It all stems back to mindset set, potentially not doing step one - The Vision, and therefore not having a clear picture of why you're doing what you're doing. People fall off or they start doing really well. They get results and then they fall off. There are also everyday life stresses that happen – things get in the way – but also it can happen because they didn't commit to it strongly enough.

Most people do networking from the home. They don't have a specific office and home is naturally your place of relaxation or escape from work. I think what happens is, people haven't set themselves up with regards to a proper schedule.

At work eventually, if you don't show up, you'll get sacked. We don't have an internal authority. That external authority (your boss) is strong enough to make us show up, then you go through our whole system, we've had it ingrained. At school you're taught, or you work for the most of the day, and then you go home.

There're many levels of authority, and I think people fall off the bandwagon if they don't have them. It's like the entrepreneur versus the employee. If we have the online business, working from home, we don't have a boss, an authority telling us what to do and we don't have pain. We're left to our own devices.

And yes, we may criticise and chastise ourselves, but that's more a perpetual cycle of victimhood. And that's a whole different topic entirely.

JC:

This is where the coach or the mentor, and plugging into events, and realizing that someone's already ahead of you... is so important!

CP:

I've seen so many people who don't utilise the support, and why?

The new person has to be proactive. If you're the new recruit, the new distributor, the whatever the label and your business, you're the one that needs to be proactive.

You're the one that needs to ask for help. I work with people who are hungry; the people who are hungry get more of my time. The people that I work with the most are the people that ask for my time and the people that reach out and show me that they're hungry. I'm committed to helping people who are committed to helping themselves.

The more commitment you show up for, the more commitment your sponsor, coach or upline will give. I spoke earlier about this: the level of commitment you give equals the level of results. You get big commitment equals big results, whereas small commitment equals small results.

There's also going to be a lot of sacrifice and you need to commit to sacrificing certain things. When I say sacrifice, everyone's going to worry that those are negative sacrifices. If you're going to change your situation, and you're going to connect to something new, then other commitments are going to have to adjust or stop.

For example, it's not something that I'd recommend, but I gave up all social life. I had zero work life balance, which is not what I recommend people do. But I am hungry and ambitious at a high level, speed is key. It's a bit of a double-edged sword, I'm saying this, because it's a 'do as I say, not as I do' approach. I was doing 12- or 14-hour days. I'd set up the computer and work so long I forgot to eat and drink. Because I could work in multiple time zones, I wasn't able to sleep due to inspiration and ideas. So, I talk about the commitment and giving up certain things, but I went extreme.

I tell people that it's a choice. You can choose to give up everything, but a sacrifice could be taking away some of your social or relaxation taken. Or, if you have extracurricular activities, you're going to have to take from somewhere to give you more time. Your schedule is going to have to change if you want to build a business. If you're really serious about achieving your vision in step one, you're going have to change things in your life. And that's going to involve sacrifice at some level, for example sleep. Seven hours of sleep will give you an extra hour of activity in the day. That's an extra hour added to your week each day, meaning 7 hours extra you've created in your week. You won't die. But how much pain are you willing to go through to achieve all the pleasure that you dreamt about in step one?

I want to bring that back in because it's important, especially in the commitment during step two. When you're making the commitment, you need to realise what you're going to shift, what you're going to change. What are you going to sacrifice? I don't necessarily like the word sacrifice because it has such a negative connotation, but what are you going to give up, to put time into your business?

Sacrifices are for a short period of time, in your first month of business, you need to give it everything that you've got – money, love and speed. The more time you can give it, the more speed you can create and then you can come off of the high gear. The analogy of a plane taking off – when's the most energy and effort needed? As soon as it starts on the runway, you need speed to take off. If the plane doesn't reach a certain speed, there's no way that it will create elevation for lift off.

It takes a lot of energy, power and movement to take off. Even after it's taken off, you still need power to elevate to the height that is required to go into cruise mode. And everything is done in 30 to 90 day bursts.

I think, go for a 30-day run. Give it your all. Say to your loved ones and your family, that for 30 days, you'll be doing this. You won't be available as much as usual because you're doing this. If you have a spouse or partner, ask for their support. If you commit to this as a single person, you're accountable to yourself, but then you go into the deeper states of the commitment.

If you have a family, I would suggest and recommend that you also commit and share your commitment with your partner. They need to know that your availability is going to change, that you're laser focused and you're going to go down this road. This is a commitment to changing things for your family.

JC:

What about giving yourself a punishment for non-performance? Do you believe in that?

CP:

The SMARTR - acronym — stipulates that every time you reach an achievement, no matter how small, you should reward yourself. The reward might be an ice cream or a movie. But, a movie might take time away from what you're doing. If it's a gift, buy yourself some jewellery or whatever it is that you like.

The reward system ties into the goals that we spoke about in the first chapter, and the vision and the pain. I don't think we need to be causing ourselves any more pain or criticising ourselves any more than we already do on an internal level. But definitely do the reward element of it.

JC:

In terms of steps, you've got the vision, you've got the team; allocate the time, put a 'do not disturb' sign to your front door, and share it with family. Talk to your upline, talk to your mentor, talk the person who introduced you to the business. Ask them what the

basics are – what do I need to be doing? What works and what doesn't work? What should I avoid? Walk in their footsteps.

CP:

Well, we're already following a calendar schedule.

I remember in school and university, we had a calendar or schedule or topics. We had a timetable. We know that will work. We have a clock in clock out timetable: we start, we finish. Whatever happens within that day, there are meetings and other tasks scheduled. On the schedule, you're adding the time that you're willing to commit to your business. So, add your business to your schedule, so it's there visually. 9am, I start work. 8am you start travelling to work and that travelling time might also be your viewing time or listening time. Get stuff written down and have it visually in front of you, and follow it.

JC:

Absolutely, I totally agree. At the end of 30 days, you'll either prove this is going to work and you're getting results, or you'll prove that you hate it and don't want to do it anymore. Either way, it'll reveal a lot. You need a routine and to take it seriously. If you can devote an entire day to it, do that. I think consistent actions are needed to consistently achieve your goals. Keep the commitment, keep the drive, do the daily things. Chip away, chip away. Believe in yourself.

CP:

It's about being professional. Like I said, it's about taking your business seriously. If you treat your business like a hobby, it's going to cost you like a hobby costs you. If you treat your business like a business, it will pay you like a business.

JC:

That's a good one. If someone was going to take one step at the end of this chapter, to cement their learning, what one thing should they do?

CP:

It's about keeping a realistic commitment. Know your limits. How much free time can you create? Label it 'business time' or whatever you want to call it. Put in the schedule either monthly, fortnightly, weekly or even daily. Remember, one of the beautiful things about being an entrepreneur and having a business is the flexibility. It doesn't need to be Monday to Friday, nine to five, you maybe have a rolling two week or three week or four before, so it's the same thing every 2, 3, 4 weeks. We have the beauty of being flexible – just watch out that you don't get lost in being flexible. Everyday changes, so schedule daily, ideally. If you're someone that can set up the whole week, set up the whole week. Again, be flexible. If something happens, and you need to change the time; change the time, but do not miss the time. If you get a phone call from your friends, and they ask you out for dinner. If it's at the time that you scheduled to do your business? Tell them no, and you're working.

Just because you're saying no doesn't mean you never get to do it. Remember, If you're in the middle of your 30 day run, you've made a commitment. All additional extracurricular activities are put to the side. Again, how serious are you?

Chapter 3 - Generating your list

CP:

What we're going to talk about in this chapter is generating your list – how to generate your list – but more importantly, I'm going to help you qualify the people that are on your list as well. Anyone that goes into the networking industry, or any sort of networking related business whether it's within the networking industry or outside, a common phrase that's always used is 'your network is your net worth'. Being able to create your list, pull out your list, that used to be the Rolodexes, in the dinosaur day.

It is crucial: who you know? Your list is your database. Your list is something that you're always adding to. You're always referring back to it. There are people that may be on your list for years before you even approach them.

JC:

And this is your list of prospects that you're going to approach about the business opportunity.

CP:

Yeah, for this opportunity and any future opportunities, whether it's networking based or whatever. Your list is the lifeblood of your business and the future of your business.

JC:

And this is this is people you know, so it's a warm list as opposed to cold prospects.

CP:

It can be everyone actually. We can break it down to warm market, so your family, friends, acquaintances, work colleagues and such, and then cold market, potentially people who you are connected to on social media, but you've got no idea who they are. You've never had communication with them, and in essence are cold contacts. You can break this all down and then segment it. But with today's world, your list is everyone you've got on your phone, everyone that's in your email address book, everyone that you've got on Facebook, LinkedIn, and Instagram. Your Christmas card list. Whatever list or platform you're using, and it'll look exactly like your little black book. Facebook allows you, on a personal profile, to have 5000 friend contacts. Straight away, that's a 5000-person database. How good those contacts are, depends on the list. And what we'll get into with the list is also getting into relationships and such. That'll be covered in the next chapter, after we qualify who we speak to.

JC:

That brings up two things. Number one: do people find this stage difficult and, if so, why? Number two: should you be prequalifying, prejudging people? Before you approach them?

CP:

Let's start with the first question.

JC:

Do people find this step difficult? Time consuming?

CP:

Some people do. It is a time-consuming exercise when you get into building your full list. But initially, do we need to build a full list? Do you need a list of 5000 people straight away? No – you can get it started with ten, twenty, fifty, a hundred, couple hundred, at least to get going. If you don't have a list of who you know, who are you going to speak to first? You're won't be doing it in a systematic and strategic way. The qualification method that we're going to explore in this chapter will help you score people like a talent scout.

JC:

I like the sound of that. I've never heard that before and this is all in the presupposition that this is a people-based personal contact relationship-based vehicle...

CP:

Yes.

JC:

Which is where a lot of the power of the model comes from, because it's people that are in your influence sphere that you're going to be working with. You'll potentially be training them, and they'll duplicate your efforts. You're kind of cloning yourself and that's where the unlimited upside potential of networking is. Is that right?

CP:

Yes. What we're going to do with this list, we're going to break it down – we're going to do a quick list. And then we're going to do the more in depth, professional list. The purpose of the quick list is so that you get started immediately. We spoke about this in the previous chapter – speed to money is important. And it's also important to get into your contacts and build your business, because your business is built with other people. So, we just take time, at the beginning, when you've got motivation and energy, and you're ready to drive it.

We go straight into study. We don't do any momentum. We don't build any results and we don't make any money. That's because at the beginning, we're doing all the coaching and the study. That's not going to motivate your contact, your prospect, your new distributor or your new team member.

The biggest way to motivate them is to show them the money. How do you show them the money? You get them started fast. So, we're going for a quick victory. We've got quick list that we do where we qualify people with two or three questions. You make a quick list –

this is people that you have in your immediate contact. It's a very warm market or mainly friends and family.

We're going to break down the first question: what is your level of influence with this person on a scale of 1 to 10? 10 is 100% - no matter what you suggest, they'll do it. For example, I'm just going to do what Chris says, or whoever you are listening to, watching or reading.

JC:

This comes with hypnotic commands – I'm going to do whatever Chris says!

CP:

Exactly! So, this quick list should only have people on it who scored an 8 out of 10 or higher.

This will be a really small number. You may only have 5 or 10 people max – if you can get up to 20, great.

After we've got the whole level of influence rated, we're going to look at what is their level of open mindedness, on a scale of 1 to 10? 10 is completely open to looking at anything and everything, and 1 being really closed off.

The third question is, what is their drive and ambition level? On a scale of 1 to 10, how ambitious are they?

These are our three questions for your close family and friends: the quick list. Total up all these scores, obviously out of 30, to see how they score overall. Then start with the people that score the highest.

If you have someone who is less than 20, you're not going to contact them. You don't to contact them – they will go into the professional list, which goes into more detail. This will help you qualify the first 5 to 10 people that you may contact. The reason why you should do that is because firstly, they're open minded, they've got a decent level of ambition, and you've got a good level of credibility with them. They're pretty much going to do whatever you're going to do. It's a little bit like peer pressure – you do what your friends are doing.

Everyone wants to be part of the community, everyone wants to be part of the tribe, everyone wants to follow the leader, so to speak. You may not be a leader yet, but as long as you've got a good relationship with someone, you're going to have some level of influence with them. And, this is just a quick list. This is a really nice way to qualify people straight away. Sometimes family aren't going to be the best ones to approach even though they'll be on the first list. It's probably friendships, because you see them more regularly and you don't have the family ties so they're less critical. Maybe. They may be more critical. It's subjective.

The first thing is looking at getting a quick list done so that you can start contacting straight away, with your sponsor or your coach. Then, we can go into a more detailed list.

Quick List Method:

	A	B	C	D	E
	Names of Close Family and Friends	Your Level of Influence with Them: Rated 1 to 10	What's Their Level of Open Mindedness: Rated 1 to 10	What's Their Drive and Ambition Level: Rate 1 to 10	Quick Probability Score
1					
2					
3					
4					
5					
6					
7					
8					
9					
10					
11					
12					
13					
14					
15					
16					
17					
18					
19					
20					

JC:

I've never heard this before. This is really interesting because I've done this exercise several times in my life, but I've never heard that pre-qualifying part of it. You've just transported me back to your car park in London, where I've been sent out with my phone to make 10 calls but don't know who to start with. I'm racking my brain thinking, "OK I've done this before, how did I do that?' Having this would have made that so much easier.

CP:

And the thing is with your quick contact list method, it's probably going to be one of three ways. It might be live, in person, and you'll see them tomorrow. Or, you can phone them straight away. Or, maybe you send a text message, an audio message on one of the different apps or whatever. You're just going to go straight into a very simple contact message. We'll get into contact methods in the next chapter.

This part of the process gets you a list of people that you can reach out to immediately when you know nothing about it.

JC:

The second question was, around pre-qualifying – the idea that you should never judge or decide on behalf of the client whether they are going to be suitable.

CP:

This is all going to be dependent on your personal relationship and knowledge of the person, especially when we go into the second more detailed list. Do not get tripped up by yourself. Avoid the whole perfectionist thing. These scales, these numbers, these qualifiers will always adjust and change. They'll adjust and change the more you get to know someone and will adjust and change with life.

Maybe something happens and now they're less open minded, or maybe something happens because they're more ambitious now, because now there's a bigger desire to achieve X, Y, Z. These scores will fluctuate. The biggest mistake that I've seen with people is they get hung up on putting a number down.

It's quite interesting. I remember when I was first introduced to qualifying my contacts, it took me two weeks to do the scoring – just to put a number down. I was so hung up with the thought that the scores were going to be really low. I had a very big self-worth response that I'm not good enough, or these scores aren't going to be high enough, which is going to be a bad score. So, it took me way back to childhood schooling – if you get a bad score, you're a C grade student, or you're not good enough. I'm not good enough.

JC:

Compared to other people

CP

Yeah.

JC:

Johnny got 7 out of 10. I got 5. Therefore, I'm not good student.

CP:

Because I had so many people on my list that I knew online and didn't know personally, I could only score them so high in each of the categories. I think it's important to share this. Because I personally experienced the fear of putting a number down on the scoring, because it was going to be a low score, meaning it was going to be a low total, meaning that I'm not going to be able to contact them, or whatever it was. It was years ago I did this so that I can't remember everything. But I want to share the story because I was one of the people that got tripped up by myself. I knew a lot of my contacts wouldn't have high numbers. It doesn't matter what the number is – it's just about getting the list done. I have this as a PDF. The PDF spreadsheet calculates everything in scores.

Quick List Method:

	Names of Close Family and Friends	Your Level of Influence with Them: Rated 1 to 10	What's Their Level of Open Mindedness: Rated 1 to 10	What's Their Drive and Ambition Level: Rate 1 to 10	Quick Probability Score
	A	B	C	D	E
1					
2					
3					
4					
5					
6					
7					
8					
9					
10					
11					
12					
13					
14					
15					
16					
17					
18					
19					
20					

I was one of those people that got tripped up by themselves. So, it doesn't matter, and the good thing is it shows you who you need to work on your relationship with. If they have a low score, it's only because you don't know them well enough. So that means you need to create a stronger relationship.

Doing this qualifying list is vital before you move onto the next stage. The second one that we're going to go into, is when it gets a little more gritty and more specific.

JC:

So, this is obligatory. This is, do not move past this point until you've done the list.

CP:

That's how I looked at it. And I didn't move forward in my business for two weeks because I was paralysed by the fear of putting a number down.

This is a sequential order. The way you're reading this book is the way that you ought to be doing these steps. Don't jump from step one to step five and back to two, then back up to seven. This is sequential. You do it in this order, because this is the order of building your business.

JC:

And this is what you'll teach your team to do as well?

CP:

Exactly. This is what you're learning so that you can pass it on and share this book with your team, this is your duplication. That's going to teach them the model that you're working from as well. Then, you can take your insights and deeper lessons to them and help them accelerate their growth in the business and, of course, in the learning as well. If you're not doing your list, then who do you contact? If you've not qualified them, who are you speaking to? How do you know whether they're going to be receptive? Do they score highly enough to hear your message? At the end of the day, you want to have someone press play on a YouTube video or a company video, or a webinar. Or, you want them to read whatever it is that you send them. They need to have scored highly enough that they will do what you suggest and recommend what you do.

You've started in your business and you're looking for people to join you. You found a new product and you want people to use it because it's very beneficial; you've found it beneficial and you want to share that with them. If they're scoring low, they're not even going to hear what you've got to say – it doesn't matter if your product turns water into wine or lead into gold. They're not ready to hear what you've got to say. It won't matter how good the opportunity, how good the product or anything that's coming out of your mouth, if the timings wrong and the scorings are off.

JC:

It's like buying a Dynorod franchise. You've got your van and you've got your uniform, but you also get a list of hot prospects as well. In any kind of business environment that would be great – this is cracking, I'm off to the races here! How hard can it be? If you look at it as a resource, is your source of income long term? It's an asset and it's worth spending time getting right.

CP:

Exactly. It's not just a list like a database – like you said, we're qualifying people. We're prioritising people; we're reorganising people. Once you go through the list, you may actually be surprised at who you should be contacting before someone else. That's the purpose of the scoring – it's going to highlight people who are higher scores than others, and it will surprise you because they'll be some people that pop up higher than others. It's a nice gauge and a guide. This is just one way of doing it.

You may have come across a number of different ways or you may not like it and you know what? Go and do what you want to do. But don't tell me this doesn't work until you try it and have failed with at least 10,000 people or 10,000 hours. Anyone that says, 'oh, I tried, and it didn't work,' – they just didn't do it enough times. They spoke to three people. We all know the numbers.

JC:

Well, on that point, I think people really underestimate the numbers.

CP:

Yes.

JC:

How many people am I actually going to have to contact before I get a bite?

CP:

Exactly.

JC:

And it's high.

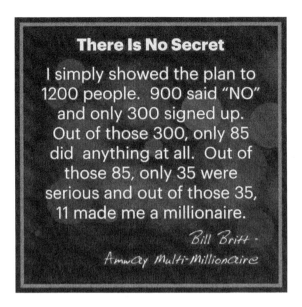

There Is No Secret

I simply showed the plan to 1200 people. 900 said "NO" and only 300 signed up. Out of those 300, only 85 did anything at all. Out of those 85, only 35 were serious and out of those 35, 11 made me a millionaire.

Bill Britt -
Amway Multi-Millionaire

CP:

Bill Britt is a multimillionaire with Amway. For those of us who are not new to the networking model, you all know what Amway is, but basically what Bill Britt said was: "There's no secret to networking or the numbers. I simply showed the plan to 1200 people. 900 of those people said no, and only 300 people signed up. Out of those 300, only 85 did anything at all. And out of those 85 only 35 were serious, and out of those 35, 11 made me a millionaire." So, Bill Britt started with 1200 and went all the way down to 11. In order to get the 11 superstars, he had to go through 1200 people who saw the presentation.

Now if we go beyond the number of people that say yes to seeing the information, you're easily looking at tripling that number, if not making it even higher.

Let's say you only get 10% of the people you speak to – that means that 1200 turns into a very high number of people you need to reach out to if you're very poor at converting. It's just numbers – speak to enough people and you'll get there.

JC:

And if you do X number of hours per day, which I'm sure you'll cover in the next chapter, it's just activity. Just focus. You're digging for gold. A lot of metaphors. You have to shovel a lot of coal before you uncover a diamond. But as one of my clients said recently, "it's not rocket science." I like that.

CP:

So, we spoke about the quick list.

JC:

Yes

CP:

Now we go into the rest of your contacts.

JC:

Will people who are on the quick list be on the other list as well?

CP:

Yes, we put everyone on it. What you'll find then is you'll get a more detailed score because we're asking more questions.

CP:

Okay, so what is your level of influence and credibility on a scale of 1 to 20. We're getting more specific with it, and we're then going to move into, what is the life timing? Is this the correct timing for them? Then again, what is their open mindedness? We're going to keep that question still 1-10 and still 1-10 on the life timing. Also, what is their level of popularity with others? If they were to do a names list, how large is theirs? You could almost split that last one or just keep it combined, but it is on a 1-10 scale.

So, we've got, what's your level of influence and credibility?

We have got, what is their life timing?

We've got what is the open mindedness?

And we've got, what is their popularity level with others? How large is their names list?

By going through your list and just one by one scoring them and totalling them up, you'll very quickly have a hot contact list. These are people who are ready to hear from you, those who you need to reach out to and find out some information so you can score them better. There are also people that you need to really build a better relationship with because you just don't have information to be able to answer the questions properly. So, this is a live, interactive, list, especially when you do it on the spreadsheet. Because the names will start to move, and the list is going to change.

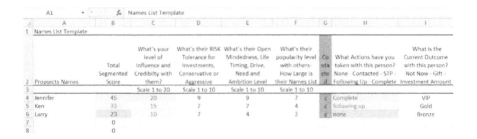

	A	B	C	D	E	F	G	H	I
	A1	▾		fx	Names List Template				
1	Names List Template								
2	Propsects Names	Total Segmented Score	What's your level of Influence and Credibilty with them?	What's their RISK Tolerance for Investments, Conservative or Aggressive	What's their Open Mindedness, Life Timing, Drive, Need and Ambition Level	What's their popularity level with others- How Large is their Names List	Co nta cte d	What Actions have you taken with this person? None - Contacted - STP - Following Up - Complete	What is the Current Outcome with this person? Not Now - Gift - Investment Amount
3			Scale 1 to 20	Scale 1 to 10	Scale 1 to 10	Scale 1 to 10			
4	Jennifer	45	20	9	9	7	c	Complete	VIP
5	Ken	33	15	7	7	4	c	following up	Gold
6	Larry	23	10	7	4	2	c	none	Bronze
7		0							
8		0							

JC:

I've seen aide memoirs where you get lists of job titles, like who do you know who's an architect? Who do you know who's an accountant?

MEMORY JOGGER

This easy memory Jogger will help you create your initial list of key friends, business contacts and others to share your product or opportunity with, so you can kick-start your NM business.

The members of your own family:
- Father and Mother
- Father-In-Law/Mother-In-Law
- Grandparents
- Children
- Brothers & Sisters
- Aunts & Uncles
- Nieces & Nephews
- Cousins

List you already have:
- Current address book/online contact manager
- Email addresses list
- Cell phone contacts
- Holidays cards list
- Wedding invite list
- Child's birthday invitee list
- Business cards list
- Social media:
  - Facebook
  - LinkedIn
  - Plaxo
  - Twitter
  - Skype
  - Other

Your closest friends and those whom you associate regularly:
- Friends & Neighbors
- People you work with
- Church members
- Hobby buddies:

- Camping friends
- Dancing class associates
- Drawing class
- Fantasy Football league friends
- Fishing buddies
- Hunting friends
- Karate class buddies
- Singing class
- Sculpting
- Woodworking friends
- Workout friends
- People with whom you play:
  - Bowling
  - Football
  - Golf
  - Racquetball
  - Tennis
  - Volleyball
  - Any other game

Those you do business with:
- Auto mechanic
- Accountant
- Banker
- Babysitter/Child care provider
- Car dealer
- Dentist (your kids too)
- Doctor (your kids too)
- Dry cleaner
- Grocer/Gas station attendant
- Hair stylist/barber
- Housekeeper

- Lawyer
- Merchants
- Pharmacist
- Real Estate Agent
- Travel Agent

Who are my ...?
- Architect
- Associations members
- Bus driver
- Butcher/Baker
- Computer Tech
- Children's friends parents
- Chiropractor
- Club members
- Delivery person
- FedEx/UPS Driver
- Fireman
- Florist
- Jeweler
- Leasing Agent
- Mailman
- Minister/Pastor & their wife
- Pet Groomer
- Photographer
- Police
- Property Manager
- Sports Team members (your kids too & their parents)
- Tailor
- Veterinarian
- Waitresses/Waiter (my favorite)
- Water Supplier

CP:

So you can use a tool if you're struggling to get a names list. To be honest, people struggle because they're getting in their own way. How many contacts do people have on their phone? How many people do they have email addresses, and how many people are on social media? I think the average number of friends people have on Facebook is near the 300 level. So, if everyone's got a contact list on Facebook at 300 people, why are you struggling to get 10 on your list? You're tripping yourself up before you even get started.

JC:

How long should somebody devote to getting the quick list and the main list done?

CP:

Quick list should take ten to twenty minutes. Who are the people that you get the biggest influence with? Mom, dad, brother, sister, and friends. So your close circle of friends – you're already into double figures, depending on how big your family is, depending on how big your social circle is. Most people have one or two people that they're close to, that you can phone immediately and say: you need to check this out, if I send you a video, will you watch it? This is one of the contacting methods, that we'll go into in the next chapter.

JC:

So, spend a decent amount of time on that, and your main list is going to be an ongoing evolving project?

CP:

You're always adding new people to your list.

You're want to always be adding to your database because you never know when the time is going to be right. Even when people tell you no, it's no for now, but not forever. No matter why someone tells you no, it doesn't matter. What it all boils down to is it's not the right timing, no matter what they ever tell you. I don't have enough time. I don't have enough money. I've just started a new job. I've got a new baby. All those reasons are saying it's not the right time.

JC:

How many times were you approached in the network that you eventually you joined?

CP:

Oh, that's a different question. The first network I joined was because of the level of influence two people had, and we were in the same professional circles. I'd known about the networking world for a good eight years before I said yes to a company, because it had to be the right company. This was based on a product company, a consumerism company and it had to align with my ethics, morals, values, and it also had to align with the business that I was already doing at the time, because it was a complimentary add on. So, I actually said yes the first time because I was looking for something that would align.

JC:

I wonder how highly you scored on their list.

CP:

Yeah, well, they knew me well enough, my ambitions were through the roof. My ambition would have been 20 instead of the 10.

Even the business that I'm extremely successful in today came from my downline, from the first business. We had a really good relationship, so I was open to looking at it. I was resistant. I'll be completely honest with all the readers and listeners. I was resistant because it was downline. And because it was moving away from what we were already building. It was another company. I wasn't ready to move away from and the company that I was working with. However, the current plan wasn't fulfilling the finance. It wasn't a massively profitable business that I was in and since I changed companies I've never looked back. So again, it was all about timing and influence.

It's all about relationships with the people that you know, I do a lot of work on social media, and I've built my business pretty much from Facebook. I know people who are successful in the networking world who I don't know personally, but I've got them on social media and they know I'm successful as well. But they're not open to hearing anything from me because they don't know me, no matter how successful I am. They have no proof of my success because they don't know me. I could turn around and say I'm a six figure earner, I'm a seven figure earner, but it doesn't matter because they don't know me and we're not in the same location for them to get to know me.

So, relationships are everything in this business. It's more relationship marketing instead of network marketing.

JC:

Okay, so as the reader goes off to do the assignment from this chapter, they'll make their list and see who's scoring highly, and there's some people who they should be approaching first. They'll have the method of approaching or methods in the next chapter, so they know what to say. It boils down to what to say and who to say it to.

CP:

It's about keeping it super simple. K-I-S-S. Avoid over complicating it.

JC:

And if they're doing a 30-day run that you talked about before, and they're batting out X number of approaches per day, then they're very quickly going to start seeing results.

CP:

Yeah, they'll start to get conversions. The main thing is, it's about getting people in front of the information. There are sales statistics to do with the number of exposures. Why do you think the same advert plays on the TV so many times? Why do you think you hear the same ad on the radio so many times? It's because people need multiple exposures of the same information before they're ready to say yes. So, say yes to the next chapter, and you'll find out how we do this.

JC:

It's like all the power companies in the world will send you a letter asking for money. If you don't give it to them, they'll send another letter. Maybe you still don't – they'll send you another one. They'll keep doing that until they get the money, and there's a lesson there. So, do the exercise, play with it, generate a list - are we going to set a target, maybe we can say X number of names.

CP:

A quick list – we can get up to 20. On your big list, easily get 100 people down and get them scored, and then do another hundred.

JC:

Excellent. So, if they don't implement this chapter...

CP:

If you're not going to do this, then how do you know who to speak to? How do you know who you're going to contact about your opportunity or product that you're offering? And how do you know it's going to be the right time to speak to them? How do you know your relationships are strong enough that they'll press play on the video or read the information you're going to send?

JC:

But, if they're willing to spend a couple of hours doing this exercise here...

CP:

You'll have a database that you can work from, and a strategy of who you're contacting and you're going to work. Do your highest ones first, and as soon as you get your highest ones done, then you can move into some more of the contacting techniques that we'll speak about in the next chapter. Then you can develop your relationships to score the people better. When I say score better, I mean score more accurately. So, then maybe they move up in the scale, but they may also move down on the scale as you find out new information about them.

JC:

Love it. I've never heard it described this way. It's a hugely powerful distinction which I really like, and if I'd been reading this book at this point, I would be thinking that was worth the price of the book just for that piece of information.

CP:

I've given a number of questions that you can ask. If you want to change it and make it more industry specific for your company, then change it. And you can add to them if you want, but do not get stuck in 'I'm going to do eight questions or 10 questions," and then you never actually get to the next chapter where we reach out and contact these people.

JC:

"I'm going to make a multicolour spreadsheet!"

Chapter 4 – Contacting

JC:

We are on chapter four of the book, which is great. And today we're talking about...

CP:

Well, you've got your list, potential prospects, warm contacts that you could expose the opportunity and invite them to. Now we're going to look at how do you do that.

Contacting...

What do you say to them? Is there a system or method? What have you found works? How do you have that conversation – do you do it on social media, on the phone, face-to-face? That's what we're talking about today.

JC:

If you can sum up the whole contact process, how do you want people to think of it? Because I think this is the part that scares people.

CP:

Yeah, okay. When you're contacting someone, when you're introducing someone to an idea, three subconscious questions will come to their mind: What's in it for me? Why should I care? And, what can I do about it?

If you address those three questions alone, without the person having to ask, they should be open to seeing what it is that you're doing.

Use that as a template in any presentation you do. You should always address those three questions.

I don't like saying 'should', but it is advisable; you'll get a much warmer response if you can answer those three questions within you're offering.

Your contact message needs to cover that , and when we go to the presentation in the next chapter, your presentation also needs to do this straight away. In your presentation, this would be your opener.

JC:

So, can you, in a contact message, tell the person what's in it for them, tell them why should they care, and what they can do about it? You're pre-empting any objections and questions that may stop them or shut them down.

CP:

These three questions should be answered in the presentation, when you're providing everything that your opportunity or project will do.

But, I also like to reference these points when I'm contacting, because it keeps me thinking about what they're asking while I'm speaking or once I've finished speaking; it helps them, but it helps me more.

I'd actually like to include this in the contact, as well as in the presentation for the next chapter. We all know we can contact people in many ways.

How are we doing it? What are our methods? We've got old-school phone call, emails, text messages, multiple different social media platforms, apps, audio messages. These are all the ways that we can contact.

There's no one perfect way to contact people; you want to cover everything; you want to cover all your bases.

Ultimately, I like to use voice, whether that's face-to-face or an audio message. I cannot convey any sort of confidence, excitement or posture in the typed or written word. No one can hear how I feel.

And if they're not face-to-face, screen-to-screen, they cannot see what's going on with my facial expressions, my gestures; I'm very animated, as you can see, I move my hands a lot, I gesture a lot, I'm very physical when I speak.

Sitting and doing these calls, I can do, but I'm much more animated when I'm on my feet. As you saw last night, Jonathan.

JC:

Yep.

CP:

So, I like to work with voice. A lot of people will avoid doing the audio message or phone call, especially phone call. Why? Because it puts them on the spot; they're stepping outside their comfort zone. But this is a business you've never done anyway, so you're already stepping out of your comfort zone. You may as well keep doing it and it's going to expand. But, back to contact methods.

JC:

Okay. So, I've got my list, I've got name, number one looking at me.

CP:

So, how are we going to contact this person?

We've already qualified whether they're warm market, an associate or someone that you're building a relationship with.

So, if you're going to contact them, we want to qualify what is going to be your message. Is your message going to be about a business opportunity? Is your message going to be about the product that you have, or the services you have available?

You need to qualify, are you going to go down the business route? Are you going to go down your product customer route?

Let's say it's a business opportunity, a business pitch, a business contact.

"I've just started a (new business) that helps people do (X). I thought of you because of (X). If I do(X - give you a video), will you do (Y - watch it)?"

Let me formulate a question there. "I've just started a new online business that helps people to generate financial freedom in three to five years. I thought of you because we've been friends for years, and if I do this, make it and leave you behind, you'll be annoyed, to say it politely.

If I sent you a video with the info, would you watch it?"

So, there are a number of things in there. One, you've told them what it is that you're doing. Two, you've told them what the objective is, what they'll achieve. And three, you've qualified why you've reached out to them.

This contact message that you just read was all based around someone who is a friend — you could just phone them up and tell them what it is.

And at the end, you do the if-I-would-you technique, so, "if I give you a video, would you watch it?"

All you're looking to do on the contact is get their eyes on the information, whether it's a video, a website, a PDF. Whatever method your presentation's on, whatever info you're sharing, that's what you want them to look at.

You're not looking for them to sign up right now. You might think that which is the mistake that most people make. They don't even get to contacting, because they have this image in their head that they need to sell people the product or the business straight away.

JC:

Yeah.

CP:

You're not selling anything yet. Even if you feel that you're not a salesman and you don't like salesmen, to be honest, we sell to each other every day anyway.

Do you like me? If you don't, then I didn't sell you me well enough. If you do like me, then I've sold you enough of me that you like me, we get on, we resonate.

So, putting the sales things to the side, all we're looking to do is get people to see the information. We want them to press play or read whatever it is you need them to read. It's the same as, "there's a new Star Wars movie out – do you want to come to the cinema with me?" Same thing.

"Hey, I've just started a new online business that helps people create financial freedom in five years. Do you want to come over to the house and I can show you some information about it, and then we can get some questions answered?" That's a different form. I just changed the template a little bit, but it's the same idea.

JC:

Yep.

CP:

Any business has got loads of acronyms, but K-I-S-S, which is Keep It Super Simple, is used a lot in the networking world. Why? Because people over think it all the time.

The people that are successful and make money in this business know the simpler it is, the bigger the success you have.

If you're on day one, week one, month one, sitting here, worrying about selling to your contact list, whether it's friends, family, people you work with, people that are in business networks, whatever circles you're wanting to bring your opportunity to, if you're sitting there over thinking it, you'll never get started.

So, the simpler it can be, the sooner you can get started with a very simple business contact pitch. You've got your business networking event – at most business networking events, you will get a 40 to 60 second pitch.

We're all there for business, we're all there to pitch what we're doing. We're there to give the bullet-point snippets in a professional, concise way, that will create the intrigue for someone to come and ask us more, or it'll be bullet-point enough, and there'll be enough information for them to go, "I know someone that needs what you're doing."

JC:

It educates them; it enables them to then introduce people to that opportunity.

CP:

It's enough to get an introduction, or to get someone to look at more information. Because once they look at the information, the decision's on them.

"Oh, no, this isn't what I thought it was, this isn't for me, but it's for Bob or John." Or, "oh, no, this isn't for me," and that's fine.

Some people will say, "Okay, I can see some good things. I'm not sure about that; I don't understand that, and I've got some questions." So, get something arranged with them, with a business partner. We'll do a BPI, a Business Partner Introduction, so there'll be three of you on the call.

Why do we do a business partner introduction? That's going to be covered in a later chapter.

That's where we get questions addressed, is with your coach, mentor, business partner, or your upline support.

It's the traditional three-way call; I think Business Partner Introduction is more traditional business language, which will be received more normally.

One of the issues that I've come across many times, and read many times, is that people are savvy to network marketing language, or MLM, multi-level marketing.

JC:

"If I could show you a way Mr Client." Alert, alert, alert! The alarm bells are going off with, "Pyramid scheme! Pyramid scheme! Pyramid scheme!" Or, I'm being sold to.

CP:

Yes, because it's a huge industry, which brings in hundreds of millions, and billions of dollars, pounds, euros, every single year.

You can guarantee that the person you've spoken to has probably been pitched a network marketing company before, and probably several times.

So, we need to have the awareness that people know about the industry, but they've been misinformed about it. When they recognise that you're speaking about something that sounds like what they've heard in the past, their alarm bells are going to go off and the doors are just going to shut and they're not going to want to hear anything.

This is why I use slightly different language, so that it's more like traditional business. This is just in reference to the three-way call language and I prefer to use business partner introduction.

JC:

It's quite possible they've been pitched badly.

CP:

Oh, yeah. Everyone's been pitched badly. Why have they been pitched badly? Because they've not had the proper coaching, mentoring or support. A lot of people dive in, and dive out even faster.

They go in with unrealistic expectations. This links into our contacting because, what are your expectations around contacting?

Just because you loved it and decided to get in and get the premium pack, the big professional one that had all the bells and whistles.

JC:

The goodies, yeah.

CP:

It doesn't mean that your friend's going to do that.

It may not be the right timing in their life for them to see or hear what your message, opportunity, project, or product, is.

When you get a "no" in contacting, the reason is it's not the right timing. It's got nothing to do with you, so don't take it personally.

This brings in all the personal development stuff. Stop thinking it's the company: it's not the company. Stop thinking it's the product: it's not the product. Stop thinking it's not a good compensation plan: it's nothing to do with compensation plan.

Stop thinking that it's not good enough. It's just not the right timing for that individual person.

JC:

Yeah.

CP:

When we're doing our list, we need to take the timing into consideration: new job, new partner, marriages, deaths, weddings, new-borns.

JC:

Moving house. Illness. Life events.

CP:

Yeah, new job, being sacked.

Financial troubles, meaning they've taking on two jobs already, and maybe looking at a third because they don't know any other way to earn money except for exchanging time for money. So, they take on a 40 hour a week job, a 10 to 15 hour a week job maybe twice, and then they're up to almost 80 hours a week.

So, have the awareness that the no just means time isn't right. This is why we do the list – to qualify people, to make sure it's the right timing. When we're contacting, we formulate our contact around this basic template.

I'm doing X, that helps people do Y. I thought of you because of Z. Then the if-I-would-you technique, or you go straight into, "I've got a 10 minute video that I can send you right now. How soon can you watch it?"

What I've just said is we've got the option for the template. You can now do the If-I-would-you, or you can go into the "I have a 10 minute video", so you're qualifying time. "I've got a 10 minute video that gives you the information you'll need."

How soon would you watch it?

JC:

How soon, not when.

CP:

Yeah.

Infinity Mastery Series Book 1

You're presupposing that they are going to watch it

You're giving them direction.

It's very purposeful language, so how soon, it's very purposeful rather than "when".

When puts it in their hands, how soon makes them think "how soon".

So, how soon can you watch it? They then need to come back to you.

If it's a 10-minute video, for example, how soon can you watch it? They're already thinking when they can have that amount of time available.

Now you can go further with it: "I've got a 10-minute video that I can send you right now, and I'll phone you back in 15 minutes."

You're being very direct there, straight to the point, and definite. Which works? Again, it depends on your level of influence, and the scoring that you got.

This is about formulating your contact message, and we've focused on a business one. We've got a product base. "I've just come across these amazing products that do X."

JC:

Benefits

CP:

Yes. Or, "I found a health and wellness company that helps people do X in Y amount of time. If I sent you some information, or I thought of you because I know you've working on this challenge." The challenge could be weight-loss, weight gain, health, sleep or skin issues, for example.

That'll be a much more personal contact and the qualifying question makes it less pitchy because you're thinking about, what is their benefit.

If you answer the question without them having to ask it, you're making them more open and receptive to hearing or seeing the information.

JC:

I think it's also worth remembering that in the previous chapter we looked at pre-qualifying the people. So, you're talking to somebody that you know, you've got some first credibility.

CP:

Well, they came up high on the scoring.

CP:

I've been involved in network marketing for years, and generally, if it's somebody I know, if I get a LinkedIn message and it talks about some kind of benefit and that's one of my goals, or it's going to help me get something I want, it's going to take a minimum amount of time, then I'll, out of just polite, civil relations, I'm just going to say, "Yeah, okay, I'll have a look at that."

I'll add that to my to do list and I'll get to it.

It needs to be gentle, soft approach.

JC:

Yeah.

CP:

If you're brand new to this, you might be using different language to usual. But, this is what I call "street language" – you can say this in the pub and not sound weird.

But you will need a template of some sort. And, yes, you're going to sound like a robot when you get started. And, yes, people are going to recognise that what you're doing is not how you normally speak.

But if they're someone close enough, close enough of a friend to you, they'll give you the benefit of the doubt.

This will become more natural to you and the template will change.

You'll always have it in the back of your mind, but maybe you skip certain parts, or you add in a little bit of your own flavour, and you make it more of your normal conversational style. But, first, you'll need to learn the ropes.

In order to do wheelies on your bike, you need to learn how to ride the bike. You can't run before you can crawl.

We've got these templates to help us.

http://whatisnetworkmarketing.co.uk/index.php/free-templates/

Use the password Fromzerotohero

Find one that rolls off the tongue and it's easy for you to say.

One of the important things is to role-play. Your coach, your upline, your mentor, whoever it is, if they don't offer role-play with you to practice your contacting pitch, and ask them for it.

JC:

Yep.

CP:

Do it in the mirror, or with parents, or family, or whatever. Another technique is if you're practising your pitch on family, or even your closest of friends, then they're going to hear what you're doing without realising that they're hearing what you're doing.

Because you're telling them, "I've just started a new business, I need to practice my elevator pitch."

It's a technique.

You're actually doing a contact, because you're going to take the template, you're going to practice it, and they're going to hear it. You'll be able to get real feedback, but at the same time, they might start to get intrigued about what you're talking about.

You can practice all the different ones. You can practice your business opportunity, your income opportunity, your product that you've got; you can practice all the different variations that you can come up with, and they can start to hear it.

And I guarantee that at some point, they'll say, "See that 10-minute video that you're offering people – can I see it?" If they're interested, they'll ask.

You're using them for real-world practice. Friends and family may be your warmest contacts, but they're also going to be the most critical and potentially the hardest. Even though they're scoring high, they've got zero filters.

You will not have the filter of a professional business contact that doesn't know you personally. When you know people personally, the filters are lower.

You're going to get shouted at, you're going to get laughed at, you're going to get ridiculed, and they're going to tell you umpteen things that you hear when you come into the network marketing world about pyramid schemes, scams, only people at the top make the money, and all these sort of comments that we get, and objections, after people see the presentations and realise what it is.

JC

That reminds me of a funny story. When I first started working with my company, and I was raving about the free BMW. And that was my pitch: "I want the BMW and I need your help." A lot of people said it's a scam, it will never happen, blah, blah, blah. Then when I showed up in the 320 M Sport 37 days later, they're going, "How much are these shakes?" I actually have this number plate on the car. It says, 'Told U So'. That could be a cover picture for Facebook, that could be so many things. Told you so, my god...business cards.

CP:

Yeah. Or using the products, whatever that may be. Whether it's a magnetic mattress that you lay on at night, whether it's a weight-loss product, doesn't matter what it is. Before and after, 90 days later, here's the benefits of this business I'm involved in.

If they say no right now, just bear in mind, once you start getting results with the company, whether it's income results or whether that's product result, you can then go back to them and very often you don't need to say a word.

They're going to say to you, "Is this something to do with that thing you talked to me about a few months ago?" And you go, "Yes, it is." And they say, "What was that video again? What was that link again?"

JC:

That's cool.

CP:

The whole point of having a script for an opening gambit, if you like, is that rather than stutter and fumble, not know what to say and feeling like an idiot, being immobilised, you now have the words to say to the contacts. You now know who to talk to you; you now know what to say.

You're contacting people typically for three reasons, and this is very important to remember – why are you contacting the person?

There are a few areas. One, you're creating a relationship, the cold contact. Two, you're re-establishing a relationship. Three, your warm market – I'm pitching them. Those are your three areas that we're looking at.

You're deciding that before you're even moving into actually contacting them, and everything that we are talking about just now is when you've decided you want to actually contact and pitch them.

If we move into the second one, which is the re-establishing a relationship – and this also includes for creating a relationship – you need to get information about them.

This goes into another acronym, which is FORM-B, so F-O-R-M-B.

F is family – how's the family?

JC:

A normal question to ask.

CP:

Yeah, how's life, how's family, how's the kids, how's your wife or husband? So, we ask how things with family are.

O is occupation. What is it you do for a living? What's your occupation?

R is recreation. What do you do for fun? What do you like to do? What are your interests, your hobbies?

M is for message. Once you know enough about the family, occupation, recreation, you've got an idea of their structure, schedule, and life. You can now message them - pitch.

Once you have that information, you can estimate a time that will statistically give you a better result. Statistically, you'll be closer to getting a yes and them looking at the information. This isn't a yes to what you're offering, because you haven't given them the information, but a yes to looking.

Once you've messaged them, the only reason you are contacting them is to book an appointment where they've seen the information and they've got questions.

Remember, if you've sent someone the information, and they say they're not interested, you don't book the appointment that follows it. You don't do the follow-up, the BPI, the business partner introduction. That is only for people who have been qualified and who have a high enough level of interest.

So, once you do this pre-qualification, this pre-follow-up, or a quick follow-up, you need to qualify whether they've actually got a high enough level of interest. Again, we're always qualifying people before we move them to the next step.

So, step three is the list. You qualify them for when you're going to contact them. Do you know enough F-O-R-M, family, occupation, recreation, to message them at the right time, that will statistically give you the highest chance of them saying yes to seeing information. Once they agree to see information, you're already moving into booking the quick follow-up, which is where you then qualify them for the BPI, the business partner introduction, which is the full follow up stage.

This is also true for if you are completely working on your own. You don't have an upline that you can reach out to, or you've not taken the time to connect to your upline, or your upline just aren't local enough for you, or don't speak the language that you speak, or they're just not active, or whatever.

This is a system of duplication, so remember if you have the mindset of I-have-to-do-everything-on-my-own, because it's only going to be done to the level and standard that I want, if I do it, you might need to go back and review why you've come into this business model.

This business model is a model of working with people and relationships, and duplication. This is the model of copy-paste; it's the franchise model.

You go into McDonald's in Hawaii, and the UK, Europe, South Africa, Australia, New Zealand, they're all the same. They're the biggest franchise in the world. Why? Because they've perfected the franchise model, the copy-paste.

It's still all the same food and I'm not going to comment on the food, but it's the same marketing, the same colouring. The layout will be strategically the same based on the space, but everything's the same right down to colouring, to the chair, to the menu.

JC:

How long the fries get cooked for.

CP:

Yeah, exactly, everything. Like 30 seconds for this then 20 seconds for that and throw it together.

That's one of the reasons for the success. They have an operations manual; they have procedures; there's what you say at the counter. Once you do that, you do this – as a flowchart, all the steps.

If you've got the capital, a 16-year-old could go in and create a McDonald's franchise and run it, and be very successful for it. That's how well McDonald's have created this copy-paste franchise model, and that's what we want to do in the networking model; we want to emulate copy-paste.

The more people that can copy success and the system, ethically and morally –without you needing to be involved, then this is the whole networking model.

Work with your level ones, who then work their level ones, and they work with their level ones, and so on and so on. That doesn't happen because it's not a perfect world, but that is the idea,

Initially you're working a lot for little in return, so that in the future, you can work a little for a lot.

Remember that what is in this can work standalone without utilising your upline, but it is in your benefit to do so. And that was the point I wanted to make there.

We spoke about re-establishing a contact and using the FORM-B, acronym – Family, Occupation, Recreation, Message, Book an appointment — for your cold market and for re-establishing a connection.

If you're just going into cold market, what you want to be looking at is how do you start a conversation?

We can go in a number of areas here, but who are you contacting and why? That's your cold-market. I still do some level of qualification, especially with social media.

My success in business has probably been 95 to 98% through Facebook, and depending what age you are, reading this book, watching this video, you might laugh, or you won't, but whatever your platform is will depend on how much interaction you can have.

Obviously, Instagram is very visually dominated; I do very little on Instagram currently, just because I do so much on Facebook and I've developed it so much.

You've got LinkedIn for the business contacts. Again, I've got a good following there. I haven't moved into it the way I have on Facebook. Just because Facebook takes up so much of my time and because that's where my strongest following is, is where my strongest influence is, and it's where people know me most, is my Facebook account.

So, I'm focusing on where people know me, and where I have credibility and influence.

Pick one or two of your platforms, learn it, and focus on it. Of course, once you're earning enough, just outsource it and get them all done.

With regards to social media, specifically social media contacting, not attraction marketing yet – that's a different topic completely – but just on how to start a conversation with any of your contacts, or new contacts.

JC:

Can I just interject here – are we looking at social media as part of your mix?

CP:

Yeah, because the easiest way to do a cold contact is find someone on social media.

You can go to business networking events or you can go to the café. There's the three foot rule; if anyone's within three foot of you, start a conversation with them. And this, what I'm about to go into, will actually cover that spectrum, it's almost that prospecting spectrum.

With your cold-market, associates, warm market, you're covering all your bases. You do it in-person, on social media, using texting and messaging, etc.

But the simplest way you start a conversation: "How're you doing?" There are two questions – the second one will follow. The basis of what I'm doing is when you ask someone a question, technically, it's reciprocal; once you've asked them, they'll do ask you.

"So, how're you doing?" I've just shown an interest in how you are. Now, some of you reading this will be like, "Yeah, but everybody does this and I ask people, that I don't even care."

That's the problem. You asked and you don't even care. You're doing stuff on autopilot and you're not present. You don't care, and that's picked up.

JC:

They feel that.

CP:

If you genuinely are interested in building your business, your financial freedom, the results from your vision boards in chapter one, and you're interested in securing your family's future financially, and you're wanting to create a completely different lifestyle, there's your motivator for, "How are you doing?"

If you don't have the energetic connection of, "I want to know how you're doing because I've got a plan for the world. I've got my empire in my mind that I'm building, and the only way for me to build this is if I care about you right now."

So, "How're you doing?" I'm doing okay, life's doing well. How are you? For most people, it's automatic, so you're going into these types of conversations that people just throw back and forward. This can be standing at a bus stop, or this can be someone you know on social media and you've sent them a message.

"Hey, just catching up, how're you doing?" It doesn't matter actually whether it's a cold-contact, a business contact like an associate, or it's a very warm-contact or a very close friend. This is the opener to starting a conversation.

If I go back to the re-establishing a connection; "how you doing?" "I'm good, how are you?" "I'm good. What's new with you? It's been a while, we haven't spoken."

"Hey, it's been ages since we've been in touch, how're you doing?" "I'm doing good, how are you?" "I'm doing really well. I've started this new business, and there's been loads happening since we last spoke. what's new with you?"

Now, there's a little bit of a template, if you read through this, you'll see a template. But what did I just do when I replied? I gave them a snippet; I gave them a crumb that I'm doing something different that they didn't know about. But I went past it and went straight to what's new with them.

JC:

Yeah.

CP:

You've already given them the crumb of what's new in your life, just enough for them to potentially be intrigued. You're going fishing, you need to use some bait. You need to get a bite.

You gave them a little bit of a bait, but then you've also asked them what's new in their life. Usually, they'll come back. If your influence and credibility in the relationship is strong enough, they'll come back and ask the same question.

If it's not, potentially they won't, or if it's a new contact, potentially they won't. However, what you've done is, you've concreted it twice.

You didn't just ask the question in the hope that this whole reciprocal thing will kick in and they'll ask you the question back.

So not only have you given them a little bit of bait to nibble on and taste, you've also asked them the question, so you've doubled up your chances of them responding to the, "What's new with you?"

And the "what's new with you?" depending on where you are at in your relationship with this person, depends on what you do it on...

And this is where it can get quite technical.

Is it your warm market? Are you re-establishing a connection? Is it someone completely new, a cold-contact? If so, you won't be asking each other what's new, because you don't know them.

But if you're re-establishing, what's new with you, they've now asked you this question.

JC:

Yeah.

CP:

There are a few ways you can respond to this. The easiest response that will build you the biggest rapport in the long-term is, "You know what, let's jump on a call and I can tell you more about it. How's your schedule this week and next week?" Or, "let's meet up for a coffee at the local."

Now, again, speed to money. What's the most efficient use of your time? Be very definite on what you're doing. Are you going to take the time to travel to the café, to be at the café, to travel back home? Calculate your time management.

Are you time rich or time poor? If you're time poor, do a video call or a phone call. Even if you're not into doing video calls, it's a great opportunity for you to stretch your comfort zone, because you will have to get used to it.

I always invite people on a video call. They come on it and if they don't switch on their video, I leave mine on. I've had people switch theirs on eventually, whether it's at the beginning or into the conversation, because I'm doing it.

Now you know this person or you're re-establishing a connection, so why would you do that? Because it's going to build rapport. You can do Family, Occupation, Recreation. You're establishing information, you're collecting information on the person so you can establish when's going to be the right time to Message – F-O-R-M.

When you message, the only reason you are doing a contact message is to book an appointment. The appointment being that they've seen the presentation, seen the information you want to give them.

Either they're interested and you get them set up with a business partner introduction, or they're not, and they go on the not interested list, which then there's a whole other thing that happens here.

So, the contact is actually quite a big area. We're using social media, text messaging, WhatsApp, whatever app you use on social media. So, how are you? What's new with you? It's a two question strategy.

This works, like I said, for establishing old relationships.

Now, for cold contacting, the majority of us have people on our social media that we do not know, that we have never met, that we will never meet unless you create the opportunity for the meeting to happen.

So, guess what? Facebook prompts us a number of times around social conditioning. That opens up the opportunity and the reason why you would send them a private message.

I specifically use Facebook, and LinkedIn has this as well. Some of the other apps or other platforms won't. Instagram won't do these things. This is why I focus on Facebook primarily – you get birthday reminders.

Whenever it's someone's birthday, there's an opportunity to private message them and start a conversation. Now you're not starting with, how are you and what's new? You're starting with, "Happy Birthday."

Now if it's a cold-contact, for re-establishing a connection, a warm-market and even people that are on your Facebook that are cold, when you've never met them and you can't even remember why you added them or how you added them, and how they're even on it. This creates a whole different chain of questions, thoughts, and actions.

But if you're building your social media for business, then you're probably adding in a lot of different people, and that's why they're there. It creates the opportunity to initiate conversation, and that conversation could lead to you initiating an introduction.

If it's their birthday, you can wish them happy birthday; the next day, my thing is to actually reach out and ask them, "So how was your birthday celebrations?" I'm starting a conversation.

They're going to tell me one of two things. They either have celebrated or they haven't yet, and that's going to lead on to my next part of the conversation.

They say that it was great, or they just spent it with family and friends. You're going to try and acknowledge the fact that you haven't had communication with them before, and you can't exactly remember how you got connected, and you ask them the question, "Do you know how we got connected?"

If this is the cold contact, the person that you don't know, it creates the intrigue. It makes them think, well, why are we connected? And that can give you an opportunity to say, "why are we connected? Was it because of the business that I'm involved in? Is it because you've seen my post and you like the content that I put out?"

You can almost dictate to them some of the answers they can respond with, and your dictation of the possible answers are also bait.

"Is it any of the posts around wealth creation that I've done? Is it any of the posts around income and how to make money? Is it any of the posts around health and wellness? Is it any of the posts around skin care?" Whatever your product may be or whatever your business is.

There's a number of people in the networking world who have previous professions, and they're adding or transitioning. There are people who don't have anything and don't use social media, so they're not putting content out there. It's going to depend on you and what you're doing.

You'll be reading this and maybe it's getting too technical, and too detailed. There're many layers to everything that you can do, but remember, I kept this very simple. Two questions: how are you? what's new with you? Happy birthday, I hope you get spoiled today, I hope you have great celebrations. They'll probably come back and thank you.

Next day, how was your birthday? I haven't celebrated yet, I'll be celebrating at the weekend with some drinks. Great, where are you going? Like where do you plan to go? Is it a big thing, is it a small thing, is it family, is it friends? Get into conversation.

The skill is developing your communication, your conversational skills – it's practice.

With the birthday one, you can't quite do the how are you? /what's new? but then you've also got memories. Every single day, you've got

Facebook memories available to you, if you've posted something, or if you connected with someone.

The beautiful thing with Facebook is it does the friend anniversary every year, and every two, three, four, five and onwards. It even gives you a button that you can click on currently, so it depends on when you're reading this.

It'll send a link as a friend anniversary post or notification and you can put a message on it. I've got a copy-paste message, which is, "Hey, would you look at that?"

And I do the tongue emoji. What does that do? Hey, would you look at that? tongue emoji, LOL, laugh out loud, and then send it. It's completely nothing, there's zero content to that.

I've even had people replying, going, "What are you on about?" And I'm like, didn't you see the message? Did you not see the friendiversary? It creates the conversation, because some people respond to messages without opening them.

Depending on whether you're on an iPhone, Android, or if you're using a smart watch or whatever. Some people just see the text and they don't see what's been linked to it. With Facebook, it links your text to a friendiversary image currently.

If they haven't opened the message, then they're probably going to question, what are you on about, because it doesn't make sense. And that's a good thing, because it's curiosity.

You're wanting a response. You're wanting them to reply and it doesn't matter because there was a reason that you messaged them, and it doesn't matter that they're confused about what you said.

You can direct them to open the message and then they go, "Oh, I didn't see that. Has it been that length of time already?" Like I can't believe that. All these sort of responses come up.

So, that's what I do with social media. This is very easy for anyone to use. Without getting technical and detailed, is you use friend anniversaries and you use birthdays.

You can do this on Facebook, and you can currently do this on LinkedIn as well. They've got business anniversaries; they've got birthdays listed. That'll depend on whether you've got those settings active or not, so that's a very simple social media one.

Birthdays and memories is good for cold-contacts. It's just people that are on your Facebook that you added and didn't get to messaging, or they looked professional and you added them because you knew at some point they'd be someone that you would want to contact.

But guess what? Once you've started that conversation, what you going to be doing? You're going to be building a relationship and getting information. How do we do that? Family, occupation, recreation, message, book an appointment — F-O-R-M-B. But you need to do enough F-O-R in order to do M, in order to do B.

If this is a cold-contact and you eventually get to, hey, how you doing, like you had a good birthday last week? How's things? They're going to say, I'm good, how's things with you? I'm doing well. Listen, we've never met before, and I do a lot of work on social media, I'm always meeting people every day, I'm a people-person, I love meeting people. I'd love to get on a call if you're open to it and find a little bit more about you, and love to get a proper introduction. You look like a very professional person, you look like a very successful person, I'd love to hear what it is that you do.

The nice thing about using an online platform like Facebook or LinkedIn is the message thread is right in front of you, so you can actually see exactly where person number one is in the process.

Exactly where person number two is in the process, and maybe for the purpose of this book, we may actually have a couple of pages and have it almost like a flowchart.

Your Messenger inbox, if we're talking Facebook, is essentially where people are at in your funnel of conversation.

And exactly what you said – it's almost like a little bit of a CRM. You already got a complete database management system.

JC:

Exactly. And it's free.

CP:

That's some very simple strategies on social media. If you want to go more into the social media side, you're going to need to give good content in order to create a following, so that's a completely different topic.

Don't expect to start putting posts out and get love straight away. Social media marketing, or social media attraction is a minimum 12 to 24 month process of value in content and consistency.

Don't think that you can jump on social media from nothing to everything. It takes time; it's the leveraging of time and the leveraging of your consistency of being seen.

If you're someone reading this and you don't want to be seen, and don't want to do social media, that's cool. No problem with that. We'll look at the other avenues. Let's go back to the list, to calling, messaging privately, going to public local events, meeting new people, however you can meet new people if you don't like your social media.

I know a number of people who are highly introverted, who have expanded their extroverted side just enough that they can be extremely successful in this business, six figure incomes, seven figure incomes. And it's just all about, how much do you want it?

At So we've covered the contact in quite amount of detail. We've covered keep it super simple, K-I-S-S.

We've covered the different methods for contacting, the different styles, we've got a template in here, we've got the F-O-R-M-B for you to collect information so that you know when is the best timing to deliver your pitch, to deliver your message and to book an appointment.

We've covered conversational skills, how to start conversation using social media, with some of the tips that I have. I haven't read these tips anywhere – this is live as we are now, with how the platform operates currently.

It's always about creating conversation; you're going to have a lot of people that don't respond, life gets in the way. People don't use Messenger if it's Facebook, people don't do this, people don't do that. People get pitched a lot.

There's always going to be the possibility of a negative there, but it's about you having consistent actions that, over a period of time, leverage the results that you get.

JC:

How many approaches a day should somebody be opening?

CP:

Can you speak to one person a day? Because that's 365 people a year. How many people for two years, for three years, for four years, for five years? Remember, if you're in this business, this is a business.

How long do you foresee yourself having this business? If you're sitting there going, "I don't have a time frame." Okay, then that's one person a day for many, many years.

That's a lot of people when you get to five years. That's a hell of a lot of people when you go get 10. So can you do one new person a day, can you do 10?

And that's not the recommended – that's your minimum.

It takes 30 seconds to type a message, do an audio message, to contact someone new on social media and go, "Hey, I really liked your profile, I hope you don't mind me connecting with you. I'd love to find out more about what it is that you're doing."

Or the typical one, which is always used in LinkedIn, and it's used in Facebook as well, is, "I am increasing my network with people of value," or, "I'm increasing my network with people who are doing well for themselves. I've seen your profile and you look like everything's working out for you."

"I want to have more people like you in my circle so that I can watch your success and potentially blah, blah, blah, whatever." It's a very common one, that I came across personally.

JC:

I've never seen that.

CP:

My LinkedIn gets spammed so much it's ridiculous.

And it's not just the blatant spam – it's usually the blatant copy-paste, I'm expanding my network, I had a look at your profile, and I wanted to add you to my circles. Even if they haven't looked at the profile.

I work 95 to 98% on Facebook, that's probably the percentage for the number of messages I don't open in LinkedIn, because they're all copy-paste spams. I haven't spent the time on it, but it's a pitch-fest.

It doesn't have the social element that I feel from Facebook. I've put a lot more time into that social element on Facebook.

So, for me, the social media is a big part of how I start conversations and how I build up being able to contact someone, because if I'm connected to them on social media, then they're on my list.

I need to get an introduction to do F-O-R, that's part of the FORM-B, to do family, occupation, recreation, to find out more about them to then answer questions on my list.

Then, as I build a relationship with them, I will strategically decide when is the right time to do M, the message, which then immediately leads to the booking of the appointment.

You're going to go slow in the beginning to go faster later on, it's like slow down to speed up.

If you've got a cold-contact and you go, "Hey, I've started this new business, do you want to come and do it with me?"

"Who are you?" So on the cold-contact side, you can't do that.

With your mate you've been going to the pub for the last 10 years with, like I've just started this new business, me and you need to work on this together because we're going to make a lot of money. If I send you a video, will you watch it? There's the template in play.

The only part of it that feels weird is if you make it feel weird. If you can say it without feeling weird, then it's not weird. The only reason why it's weird is because it's not practised, and you're not used to saying it.

So, as an action step – now is the time to get busy. It is a numbers game, so the more approaches you make, the more likely you are to hit your goals.

You asked how many people, and I said one a day. That's the simple thing, but 10 or 20 people – it's not difficult to do if it only takes two minutes each.

10 people a day, two minutes each, for each message, audio message or phone call. If it's two minutes and it's 10 people, it's 20 minutes a day.

That still gives you time for learning and other elements within your business that we spoke about, or that we will be speaking about in the following chapters: study, personal development, learning, website, back office, and learning product knowledge.

You can easily get 10 people. For 20 people, then it's 40 minutes. I mean, most people can do half an hour to an hour a day on their business – that's on the side or a full-time job – easily.

I always suggest that people keep copy and paste messages in their notes app.

It's literally copy-paste, copy-paste. Sitting, watching your favourite soap opera, start sending them messages.

http://whatisnetworkmarketing.co.uk/index.php/free-templates/

Use the password Fromzerotohero

CP:

The phone call template is all about qualifying time. You want to make sure they realise you don't have any time, so that they can't get the opportunity to get in your conversation and ask questions. Time's money, so you want to do a one-minute call or two-minute call. On and then off.

Now, warm-market, someone you can call up, "Hey, how you doing? Is now a good time to speak?" First step, qualify the time. If they say yes? Great. "I'm really busy right now, but I wanted to give you a quick call." You've just stated your time availability, so now they can't get into it, and if they try to, you can reference back.

So, "Hey, how you doing? Is now a good time we chat?" Yes. "Great, I've only got a couple of minutes because I'm really busy right now, but I wanted to..."

"Hey, how you doing, is now a good time to speak?" Yes. "Great, I've only got a couple of minutes, I've just started, or I've just done X."

So this is where your business pitch comes in for the text then the phone call.

So, I've just started a new online business that helps people increase their income. This is a crap one. It'll have their pyramid sirens going off in their head! So, I've just started an online business that helps people do X-

JC:

The end result, yeah.

CP:

Yeah. In Y amount of time.

I thought of you because of Z.

I've got a video that's 10 minutes long, 20 minutes long, 30 minutes long, if I sent you it now, would you watch it?

Then they say yes or no, and now obviously there's going to be interaction here, but I'm keeping this simple.

Yes or no, and you say, "Great, I'll call you back in 15 minutes, 25 minutes, 35 minutes." They're watching it now, and then you qualify them for what we'll go into in a later chapter – the follow-up, because the presentation is your video.

So, there's the phone one. Now, I did the "I've got a 10 minute video, a 20 minute video, a 30 minute video" element. The other side of it is you can do the If-I-send-you-would-you-watch, and then they're going to go, "Yeah, I'll do that." Great, it's 10 minutes long, I'll call you back in 15.

Again, you're now forcing them to watch it now. Now the responses that will come in will be, "Well, no, I can't watch it now." Okay, how soon can you watch it? I can call you tonight at 8:00 PM. So, again, you're still dictating and in control of the timing, so you're telling them when you can call them; meaning they need to watch it by that time.

JC:

Yeah.

CP:

For some people, this might seem pushy. It'll only seem pushy if it's more direct than you're used to being, so you need to find something that fits with your natural flow, or just a little bit outside of your comfort zone, in order for you to feel that you can do this.

Because I have a very direct personality, I have no trouble dictating to people all day long.

JC:

Yes, Chris.

CP:

But I know people who need a softer approach. They don't have anywhere near the level of directness that I have, and they will never be, and that's fine.

You need to find a way of forming this template and using your normal style. Firstly, so it's not too different for your friend that you're contacting, the person that you know, your warm market.

And, it's also close enough to your comfort level that you'll do it, because if I'm telling you something and you just don't do it, then there's no point. We need to find what you can do that's just out of the comfort zone, because if it's too much out of it, you're not going to do it.

Ultimately, if you're coming into this business for the first time, it's all going to be outside your comfort zone. You have to be willing to do things that you've never done before, and you have to be willing to push your level of comfort.

So, there's the template for a phone call. People can hear your posture, your confidence, your excitement. You can vary your tone, your influx up and down, which is where you go up, or where you go down. Now obviously reading this, you're not going to understand that.

Use the template as the foundation. They'll always evolve, they'll always change; you'll improve on what I've just said. Why? Because it'll be you doing it.

When you're doing this, when it's natural, when it's comfortable, when you're confident, when you've found your flow, you'll be doing it better than what this book is showing you, because you've learnt the skill of how to pitch and how to contact with a frame.

You've got a phone contact, you've got a text contact, you've got a social media contact.

I think face-to-face first, phone second, social media third, text and email. With letters, you're losing your energy and impact.

It's daily activity; it's building your business. If you're recruiting staff to work in your new company, you wouldn't go in with a can't-be-bothered attitude; you'd be actively looking for the superstars who are going to run with this. You're excited, enthusiastic, and that will carry over.

Your collection of information through the Family, Occupation, Recreations, is like interviewing people without them knowing they're being interviewed.

JC:

Yeah. Stealth.

CP:

If you're being direct and it is a very upfront business contact, business prospect, business pitch, then go in with the mind of like what you just said – this is a six-figure job.

What would you expect someone to do in your business if you were going to pay them a six figure salary? What skills would you expect them to have? What commitment would you expect them to have?

What personal development/professional development would you expect them to have throughout the time of their career? Try and see the other side of the coin. If this is a business that can pay high five figures, six figures, seven figures a year, or even a month, what is the expectation of the potential employee if you come from a traditional business point where you're going to hire someone and pay them a salary?

Have that mindset and you'll go into a contacting/interviewing mode a lot more easily.

Remember role-play. Pretend you're the CEO of a FTSE 100, and you're employing someone of extremely high calibre or you're seeking someone of extremely high calibre. Seek out those superstars for your business. You don't have to get it perfect; you just need to get it going.

If you jump forward in time and picture yourself six months from now where you're training your team to do the same process, and to cut and paste and to duplicate, and now you may have 10, 20, 30, 50, 100 people all doing the same process.

Think of the reach that has. Think of the exposure; your business is now getting to people. That's the strength of network marketing. That's the multiplicity part and where the geometric growth comes in. So get it done, make some mistakes, be willing to fluff it a couple times.

You'll get there.

JC:

Fail forwards.

CP:

No one died from having a conversation. Well, maybe. Get busy, because the sooner you start, the sooner you can start seeing results, and of course those results then feed your belief in the whole thing, and therefore you're more powerful.

JC:

The perpetual cycle gets going, but you're the one that needs to start the cog.

CP:

You're the driver, absolutely. So, easy, quick, convenient, simple. Don't over complicate it, follow the system, follow the steps. Go out there, start talking to people, and good things will start coming into your future.

There are many layers and if you're at the beginning, you're in the top layer. It keeps going, just like an onion – multiple, multiple layers. Keep it super simple, avoid over complicating it, avoid jumping ahead of where you're at.

Stick to where your starting point is and gradually take the steps to move forward at your pace and speed, with actions that are realistic for you to achieve. If you set expectations for yourself that are unrealistic, you'll never get started. You're paralysing yourself before you even started.

The one thing I would say is just keep it simple, one step at a time, start focusing on the smaller tasks and smaller actions which will accumulate to the bigger result.

Chapter 5 – Presentation

CP:

You've been out there approaching people and asking them, "can I share this with you? I have something really exciting I'd like you to look at." Now, they've said yes, and you're like, oh heck, now what?

What are you showing them? What is your presentation?

This has changed over the years, from before I was even doing networking. It used to be more old school, in person. You had a folder or a flip chart with a presentation that you did one-on-one. You might have gone to a local event or a company event, which is still very much the case. But it used to involve driving to someone to give them a presentation in person. Today, we've got YouTube videos. We've got many platforms for videos. You get the corporate presentation, whether it's PDF format or a video, and you're really just sending it to your contact.

Always remember, if you are making your own version of the presentation, you ought to get it approved by your company compliance department. You can do your own, you can reference from the company's materials, but before you go out there, you always want to have the company compliance sign off.

So once you have a presentation, you simply email, text message, or however you're sending it. If it's a 10, 20- or 30-minute video, always give the best video with the most concise information, that's going to take up the least amount of their time. As we all know, people's attention spans are small. So you're giving it to them. It's really simple. The presentation's already done, but if you're making your own, this is when it comes into those three subconscious questions that I mentioned previously. What's in it for me? Why should I care? And, what can I do about it? If you are going to make your own, those three questions need to be answered within the presentation.

If you're bold enough and want to be extremely direct, you'll bring these three questions, subconscious questions to the conscious level and state it. "You're probably all here wondering, what's in it for me? Why should I care and what do I really need to do about it to get started? And that's what we're going to cover today." So your presentation can be your opener, because it's addressing those three topics straight away. When you are building a presentation that's going to be sent to compliance to be approved, the way you would break it down as with the four Ps.

The four Ps are: project, product, plan, and program. So, what is the project, what's the bigger version? What is the actual product that you're selling? What is the plan? The plan is the compensation. How am I paid for what I'm doing? And what's the program, to take it out to the masses for duplication?

If you can chunk it down to, am I addressing three subconscious questions, and am I covering the four Ps within my whole opportunity?

Number one, project. Number two is product. Number three is plan. And number four is the program. Move through those areas as a template for what you are going to say, and when you're going to say it. Today, most people use the easiest, quickest way, which is to use what the company's giving you. If the company's one is boring or too long or does not convey the information in the best way, change it. But again, always come back to compliance on your presentations.

You can make your PowerPoint, you can share it with your team, you can put your personal story into it, yada, yada, yada. But you've also got presentations in your local groups, or the live event country events or national events. You'll have the opportunity to be a speaker, but you don't have to take it. Remember, the spotlight doesn't need to be on you. You don't need to take up that spotlight, but it's there if you want it. If you do, you're doing something above and beyond the comfort levels of many people. I believe the fear of public speaking is number one fear. Am I correct, Jonathan?

JC:

Before death.

CP:

Before death, exactly. The fear of public speaking. The irony is that I really like being on stage and speaking.

JC:

Do you?

CP:

I do indeed. Imagine that. The irony is that I actually dropped out of college during my last year because the main focus of that year was giving a 20-minute talk on your project. I did a full year without any intention of completing that course. I did every other module, every other unit, every other class, and finished the year without the qualification. And the irony is I did that when I was 20 and now, I really thrive on being up in front. I like the banter back and forth. I like the theatre element of it. And yes, I get a little bit of jitters and anxiety beforehand, but I actually really enjoy it and I go into a speaker mode where I almost forget everything that I'm saying, and I'm speaking without knowing consciously what I'm saying.

It's like, you become a channel of information and it just flows. So you don't need to be the person that's got the spotlight on them, but I do find it quite ironic that what I feared the most when I was at college is now what I'm doing.

But in essence, the presentation, that's this chapter. It's really short because nowadays, companies are predominantly doing it all for us. Those who are in the industry the longest are the ones who are used to maybe making slight variations and developing their own presentation.

As a way of differentiating yourself from others, and to stand out from the crowd, brand and deliver your own presentation. Remember, though to use the three subconscious questions and the four Ps to build it. You'll be off to a good start.

The good news, as somebody who's starting a networking marketing company opportunity from scratch, there already exists a complete sales message. It's already done for you. All you need to do is get as many people as you possibly can who are qualified to see it. Some of them won't be invested. Some of them are going to love it. Some of them will be somewhere in the middle.

The other thing is we're able to touch back on is duplication. As I just said, I enjoy standing up on stage or in front of a crowd and delivering the knowledge that I've gained and the company that I'm in, because I'm passionate about it. But I just told you that the number one fear above death is fear of public speaking. So how duplicatable is it, if I'm doing that and expecting my team to do it. When you're watching this, or if you're reading this, realise that not being up at the front of the stage is actually a good thing because it shows your contact that anybody can do what you're doing. Anybody can send a video or message a PDF presentation.

On a duplication level, the less you stand out, the more duplicatable it is on a general scale. You might have dreams and aspirations to be on stage, and that's fine. It's not the case that if you're out on stage, your team won't follow you. They will just like that you're doing it because they've got no interest in it. I'm just showing both sides of the coin here. You can be that person, but you do not need to be, because your coach, your mentor, your upline, your sponsor, will be that person who does that for you to support you. It will be your choice whether you choose to take the route of stepping up to that leadership role. Not a lot of people do it and it's not suitable for a lot of people either. It just depends what you want. In this chapter, it's really about just knowing that it's there, and knowing both sides of the coin – what's available to you, and that you don't have to step up in front of anyone and be in the spotlight.

It can be fun, though. I had a moment in 2017 – a very big professional development moment – which was the turning point of my liking being in front of an audience. I recognised that I stopped caring. There was this moment where my perfectionism decreased, and I shared this vulnerability. Previously, I always had to be perfect – as I put my clothes on, they had to be perfect. The hair had to be perfect. I needed to look perfect. Social situations or not, I would normally avoid any sort of photography for social media posting, because I had to be well posed for each photo. Then something happened during one of the company events that was held for the country. I was part of a team that did a little bit of role play, a little bit of theatre, just for fun.

I really enjoyed it and the more of a fool I made of myself, the more I enjoyed it. At that moment, I started to become more comfortable with not being perfect. I started to become more comfortable with photography for social media, and it just kept going. I think it was at that point I was starting to do more presentations and on my own, whether it was one-to-one or one to many. It was just a personal development moment where I stopped criticising myself and I gave myself a little bit of a break; the perfectionism dropped a bit.

I started to actually play with stupidity on social media pictures, actually purposefully looking silly, purposefully making a face, purposely not looking perfect when a picture was taken, or when the video was recorded. I decided to bring out the playful side – let's be real, be honest, nobody looks perfect all the time. And there's a lot of energy and effort and stress that's created within the physiological system when you try and live up to that expectation all the time, because it just cannot be done.

This chapter is a little bit different. It's moving into personal development and mindset. But I think it'll be very good for you reading this to read these words, or to hear these words, if you're listening to it or watching the video.

I hope you get benefit from me sharing my own personal experience there, because a lot of people have that same thing, especially with the imagery that we're exposed to of everyone needs to have the perfect face, the perfect body, perfect skin, yada, yada, yada.

JC:

Good luck with that. You'll be a long time striving for that! Okay, so tell me about napkins.

CP:

Napkin presentation is something that you can do fairly quickly. It can be a powerful presentation to someone because you're able to show it by writing it down on a beer napkin, for example, or a coffee napkin. The 45 Second Presentation is a book by Don... can never remember, Don Failla. If you look up the 45 second Presentation, you'll find it.

There's a number of those videos on YouTube as well. In essence, it's a way of doing a very brief two to three-minute presentation in which the person you're presenting to gets it straight away.

For example, the compound effect of one person brings in two. Those two people bring in two each, and it keeps going. So, your numbers double every week. 1 becomes 2, 4, 8, 16, 32, 64, 120, so on and so on. And you do that for a 30-day period or a 12-week period, you will quickly see that one person, that speaks to two people – and those two people do the same thing – by 30, 31 days, it's more than 4,000 people.

If you can show that duplication, if you can show that compound effect on a napkin, it can be a very powerful way to demonstrate how quickly a team can build. Then, you could simply do, instead of two, what would happen if it was three? And then you are working on the numbers on three and you'll see that just one extra person a week has a huge impact on the total number by time you get to 12 weeks, for example. That's one method of using a napkin to look at how our business system works. It's got a compounding system within a duplication model.

Another thing is, how quickly does your income grow? Remember, the quickest way to have success is to show people speed to money. Utilising your compensation plan, look at what the sweet spots are, which get the most bonuses, the most commissions that generate the most units, points, group volume, whatever it is you're working on. Then tie it in with the compound model and know your numbers. How quickly can your prospect get back the money that it cost them to start the business? After investing 500 bucks, 1000 bucks, how quickly can they get that back and start moving into profit? If we go back to step one with the vision and the goals, one of the first short term goals, ideally in 30 days, can we get your money back? Everyone can manage 30 days, they use a credit card, get the money back in 30 days, pay off the credit card. There's no interest on it then.

This is showing someone how quickly they can get their money back. It's showing them how quickly money can be made, and it's showing them how easily the numbers are worked. Because everything in the network and industry is about numbers.

If you can create a napkin presentation, working with just those two things, what's your sweet spots, how quickly can you make money, and then reference it with a compound of a duplication, both two people a week, three people or five, and then just do the math and work it out. In short, if you can do that or have your upline go through this with you, you can do it. You just need to learn how to deliver it.

Those little napkin presentations or something that you could do anywhere. And actually they can sometimes be a little bit of fun because it's not on a computer screen. It's not up on a projector. It's not a professional PDF. And it's duplicatable because as long as you can learn the numbers, memorize them, do the math, use a calculator on your phone, you can do a five minute, two minute, three minute, napkin presentation. If you don't have one, ask your upline. Find out if there is one and if not, can someone make it.

We're coming to the keep it super simple acronym, KISS. The simpler it looks, then the greater belief a completely new person will have that they can do it. If you can sit at a table, a restaurant, or a bar and write stuff on, write information, write numbers on a napkin, people think, I can do that. That's easy. I don't need a projector, I don't need a laptop, don't need a computer, don't even have to stand up in front of folk. I can literally sit at the pub, have a drink. If I get to talking to the person next to me, I can pull up the beer mat or a napkin and start to do a presentation.

Or if you're flying. I know a number of people that specifically choose to sit in the middle seats because they've got the opportunity to have two people for an hour next to them. It's little strategies and little thoughts like that. If you're talking to one person on a plane, the other person can't not hear it.

JC:

I like that. It's funny because you reminded me, I once hired a hotel room, and I had 40, 50 chairs laid out. I had my presentation on my laptop, all ready to go. I had a go at marketing it but I admittedly didn't do it very well, and one person showed up. One whole person. I was ready to pack up and leave and one person showed up. They walked in and it was a guy that I knew really well, and I said what do you want to do? Do you want to put this thing on and watch it? Or do you want to just call it quits and we'll talk about it at the bar? No, no, put it on and I'll watch the whole thing. So he basically sat and watched the whole 30 minute presentation video. At the end of it, he came round and said, well, what's the top package? And I said, it's this one. He said, great, I want four of them. What? He signed up four of his managers and they became his immediate down line, and we were off. The moral of that story is, you never know. You never know – its numbers, numbers, numbers.

CP:

Yeah, the right people will come in at the right time. There are many stories like yours, where a handful of people showed up to a room that should have been hundreds and everyone but one walked away thinking it was a scam, pyramid scheme, but that one person stayed, saw the vision, could see how it could be applied immediately, came in and ended up being a rock star for your team.

It doesn't matter how many people show up. It matters how many people sign up.

JC:

Yep. I don't know if you'll agree with this, that nothing's happening in your business unless someone's purchasing a product or they're signing up. Today, if you didn't get a sign up or you didn't get a product sale, then nothing happened in your shop today.

That's a wasted day. Getting this in front of as many people as you possibly can, some will want to be customers, some will want to be distributors, promoters. The best promoters are usually satisfied customers, who then see that they can actually make a living from marketing something that they already know, believe in, and have results with. In fact, they make the ideal evangelists because they are living products or the product. So sure, okay, anything else on presentations?

CP:

I was going to reference back to the contact there. When you say, if you've not sold anything in a day that it's been a wasted day of business, it's the same for contacting. If you're not contacting anyone, then it's as if you've got a bricks and mortar business and the sign on your shop front door has still remained closed and you never opened it for business. So, that analogy that you gave can also be adapted to the contact. If you're not speaking to at least one person a day, your business was never opened.

JC:

You're still paying the rent and rates and water and everything else. So, the reader of this, the watcher of this, can visualise themselves approaching people, then somebody says, yeah, send me the video, and now they're watching. They're seeing a presentation that you don't even need to give. Just send it off and let them watch it, and then you follow up.

CP:

Yeah, if you're sending them a presentation, you want to schedule the follow-up meeting or the follow-up call, ideally before they've watched it. Some people will commit to watching it and then they don't, some people say, just send it to me and I'll get to it when I want to. And this is a position, where confidence and posture, experience and belief, are all factors. When you just start off, you were like, yeah, I'll just send it to you then.

JC:

You're off the hook.

CP:

The first thing they'll say is, oh, I haven't watched it yet, or I have, or I was too busy, I forgot – these things. If you can send them the presentation and get them to commit to a time where you will then be back in touch with them, it's like another appointment. Get that confirmation, get that commitment from them, then there is a higher chance of them watching it, which means you can move into the follow up, which is what we'll cover in the next chapter.

It's exciting knowing that three people are going to watch your presentation tonight. You're following up with them tomorrow, and you put calls in your diary books to just ask, how was it? It's even better when somebody texts you and goes, I'm in, or tell me more. That's a monumental shift in your business.

Some people trip up here – they made the lists, they've done all the steps, they got their vision, they've made their commitment to how much time of spending on studying, and on building the business, they made the list of qualified people. They've contacted them, they're now sending the presentation, but, they do not set the follow up call.

JC:

Yeah.

CP:

If you're not going to follow up with people, which we're going to get into, the follow up is where you find out if they're interested or not, and when you close.

JC:

Yep. Just dropped the ball. It's key to get the presentation to them and schedule the next call.

CP:

Yeah, who knows what happens next. You have no idea what they're thinking, you have no idea who they know, and you have no idea where that's going to go. That's the exciting part and sometimes you're going to be dismissive – some people you would never expect, turn out to be rock stars. Some people you think will be rock stars end up doing nothing.

No expectations. Just because they've said yes to seeing the presentation or looking at the information does not mean they're going to say yes after they've seen it. You need to stay emotionally balanced, having no attachment to a yes or no. Remember what I said early on – a no just means it's not the right time. I've had people come back to me two years after and say, are you still doing X? And I said, yes. And they came in at the top pack. So have no expectations, because no just means no for now, not forever. You can always follow up with them when there's an update in your company.

JC:

Love it. So, if you're reading this right now, get that presentation in front of people and make sure you tell them that you'll speak again tomorrow or ask them to give you a call when they've watched it.

CP:

Follow the template, and the contact strategy. If you've forgotten what it was, or if you skipped over it, go back to it.

JC:

Absolutely. The recipe works – follow the recipe.

Chapter 6 – Follow Up

JC:

We've looked at the vision; we've looked at being committed to timing the schedule; we've looked at list building; we've looked at how you contact people and what the presentation is when you show them. Now we are into the world of following up.

CP:

Yes, indeed.

JC:

The fortune is in the follow up, as people say. Give me a big picture sum up for this chapter. Why is follow up important?

CP:

Follow up is probably more important than your contact and more important than your presentation. Follow up is where you find out what level of interest a person has, and what potential concerns and objections they have, and you get to address them.

Following the traditional model, which ideally, we all should be, aim for consolidated duplication. It's based on the BPI, the Business

Partner Introduction, which is traditionally known as the three-way call.

As we spoke about before, we pre-follow up the follow up. There is no point arranging a Business Partner Introduction call if the person is not interested after seeing the presentation. If they are low on a scale of 1 to 10 in the level of interest, say a 4 or lower, you don't want to bring them on a follow up call because they're not interested. You need to qualify the follow up calls.

There's preparation before the follow up. This is what we spoke about in the contact message. You schedule that follow up before you've even given them the presentation. That way, you have a commitment from them, and they show they are genuinely interested in taking a look.

When that pre-follow up is done, you can have your upline ready to come on a call if they're interested. Tell the contact, it's a quick two-minute phone call, to hear what they've got to say. They're interested, and they've got some questions. As they agree, tell them you'll arrange a call with your coach because they will be able to answer any questions. Again, we'll get strategies and the best language, how to best to give that message so that they actually agree to the next call.

There are two ways of having that pre-contact set up: you can either have your upline ready to come on it, or you can then set up an additional call. The latter is a bit of a longer process. It's another step and another appointment, but that's where we're at with it.

Once we get the follow up, there are now steps within the follow up. One is to qualify where they're at. I don't ask them," What did you think about the information?" I ask them, "What did you like about it?" This gears the conversation towards a positive outcome.

"What did you like most? What really stood out to you that you were impressed with?" You want to formulate the question around a positive thought process.

This is all good, but even when you ask the question that specifically keeps them positive, you can still get someone coming back with, "well, I didn't like this blah, blah." They will still do it. I respond to that with, "Okay, that's really interesting but tell me what you did actually like" with emphasis on "did" and "like", tell me what you did like. "That's a really interesting point. We'll get into that but tell me what you did enjoy." I always try my very best to redo it. I ask the question again. Sometimes they still come back with a negative, or they're like a dog with a bone and go back to their original negative point. Then I'll do it a third time and I'll rephrase it again to try and get the positive.

You want to do that so you know what they like, then you can focus and expand on it and give different points and perspectives of that positive element that they've seen. The first part is always trying to find out what they liked best. The second part is finding out the level of entry. "On a scale of 1 to 10, if 10 is I'm all in, let's go right now, what number would you give yourself?" That's the second part – the level of interest. When you've got their number, the question that follows that is, "great, that's a perfect place to be – what questions or concerns can I address to make you a 10? Again, the language is very specific around, "how can I make you a 10 out of 10?" At that point, they'll bring up their objections and concerns.

If they don't have any, ask, "why are you only a 7 and not a 10?" Is it because naturally they're a reserved person and never an 8 or a 10 in anything? Whatever the number is, it's always a great response. You never say, "oh, why are you so low, a 6 or 7?" It's always, "that's a great number to be at," whatever the answer is.

We acknowledge, we build that up, and we encourage them to share where the gap is. At that point, they'll either say they've got some questions or some concerns. Going back to those two routes, you either address the objections and concerns, or you create the three-way call.

Creating the three-way call, you'd say, "Great, you've brought up some really valid questions, some really valid points there. Because I've just started, the next thing we do is to introduce you to my coach, business partner, or senior director. They've been doing this for X amount of years, and they'll be able to address every question you have." It can end there, or you can add another layer and say, "And this is something I like to do, especially with new people."

When I hear from teams that I've worked with, it's very difficult to get people on a three-way call. People don't want to speak to strangers – why do I need to speak to your coach or your business partner? To eliminate this objection, say, "you would really be helping me out by coming on this call to get your questions answered, because I've just started. You get your answers and I get a coaching session. So, will you help me out?"

If it's a personal contact friend, family, even work colleague, there's going to be an element on a subconscious level of not wanting to say "no" to helping you and your new business. This works especially if you really lay it on, and say, "you'd be doing me a massive favour because I've just started, I am learning the ropes. Regardless of what you decide to do, this call is crucial for my coaching and you'd really be helping me." Now, you can really lay it on or you can keep it superficial, but as I said, if they're a friend, family member or colleague, they're less likely to say "no", and more likely to say "yes" with that additional element on it.

If they want their questions and objections addressed, that's the next step. We're not asking them. We actually dictate: "great, the next step is…" The quick qualifier, the quick follow up is, "what did you like best? What's your level of interest?" Follow up is where you have your BPI, where specifically it happens during the call. Or, if you are flying solo, then you're the person that's been stepping in to deal with the objections. We've got a technique for that as well of course, which is the Feel, Felt, Found.

Example - I know how do you feel? Many people felt the same when they first were introduced to this information, but what they found out when I give them XYZ information is…, or, what they found out when we spoke in more detail was the following XYZ.

You're making it more credible by utilising Feel, Felt, Found. You can go a little deeper, and not challenge the objection but overcome the objection. People are objecting because they're a little fearful, a little sceptical. So, either reference yourself or others: "I know how you feel. I felt the same way, but what I found out was, the more I dug into this project, the more I dug into these products, the more I dug into this company, it was the opposite of whatever the objection is."

The usual objection: "it's a pyramid scheme." So, you can say, "once I looked into this deeper, I understood that this pyramid scheme thing isnt illegal. It's just a structure within a business system. When I look at my own place of work, well, the same structures are in place to be honest. Every single person above me earns more, but when I looked into this system, actually, John, who was sponsored by William – John's actually earning more than William is. I had to ask the question, "Well, why is that?" It's because John's actually working in the business more than William,; John is performing, William is not. Then I came to the realisation that it was all performance compared to the employee model, as you're getting paid to exchange your time and the further up the ranks you go, the higher you get paid. Therefore, everyone above you is earning more than you, but not in this system. That got me really curious."

That's a long-winded answer, but you can see how you can elaborate and go into detail. The Feel, Felt, Found, is how we can deal with the objections that come up. Also, any objections that come up, we acknowledge them and say, "that's a great point. I'm happy that you mentioned that. I'm happy that that was part of your thinking because..." Now, what's happening at that stage is that they're not expecting you to be happy about the objection. It creates a little bit of a zap in the mains, a little bit of a system error, because they didn't expect you to be happy about them being sceptical or negative or to have an objection. It lets the subconscious wall drop, shall we say.

You acknowledge what is and then you ask, what exactly do you mean by that? Let's say, you come back to the pyramid scheme objection, which is very common, so, "what exactly do you know about pyramid schemes? What's your definition of a pyramid scheme? Tell me what you mean when you say that?" Because, for you to properly deal with that objection, you need to know exactly what they mean when they say it. "Is it just because it's in the structure of a triangle or in the shape of a pattern? Is that what it is? The person above you always earns more? You mean, like your supervisor and like their manager and then the owner?"

Whether you're in the medical system, police system, fire system, political system, any system, restaurants, franchisees…

JC:

The hierarchy.

CP:

There's always a hierarchy. With a hierarchy comes different levels of pay. The teller at bank does not get paid what the store manager gets paid, or regional manager and so on. There's a bit of education needed. The pyramid scheme is a stereotypical one. We could use a number of examples here, but it's about acknowledging their answer regardless of what it is, and then asking for specifics. Ask them, "what do you mean? Why do you say that? Why do you think this is X?" "Oh, it's because when I use google, it says it's a scam." "So, what are you doing currently that is like what I'm offering you, because if you have no knowledge about how this system, this industry, this product works, why are you just going to take the very first thing that comes up in Google?"

If you google 'your local political system is a scam' or 'your local police service or fire brigade or NHS, medical world, any company, and if you put scam' or 'iPhone and scam', you'll find whatever you're looking for. If you're looking for a scam, guess what? You're going to find a scam, regardless if it is correct or not. If you're looking for objections and negativity, you going to find that. That is the way to overcome objections and to deal with objections.

Now, the next step after dealing with objections is to ask, "do you have any more questions? Or are you ready to get started?" This is a closing question, which is key, and your complete follow up. You're giving them the opportunity to ask more questions, and if they say yes, they're not ready to sign up for the free account, for the minimum account, or to do any sort of sign up or purchase. If they are, you say, "are you ready to get started?"

Most people will either say yes or no. On the odd occasion, you get the, "I need to go and think about it," which means you've not dealt with the objections. They are not convinced that's the right thing for them, and this is when it gets uncomfortable for you, especially as a new person. Most people would say, "okay, let me know." That's because you've got to the stage where you're uncomfortable about continuing to ask them more questions. I got into the habit of asking the question, "Oh, great, you've got more questions. What is it you're thinking about that I can help you with right now."

Now, they're in that uncomfortable position because they are politely trying to say no. All you want is a yes or a no. You don't want that middle ground because this is what will cost you more money or time, because you're going back and forth and chasing them. The biggest issue around Multi Level Marketing, MLM network marketing, is everyone's anti Sales. The sales pitch is always seen as the pressured approach. In other words, if the prospect were completely honest and upfront and said, "no, this isn't for me," you wouldn't be doing the follow up call. Why? Because the prospect said it's not for them, instead they are saying, "Oh, let me go and think about it." Well, guess what? If you give them time you need to continue to follow up until they do give you a straight answer.

As far as being professional in the networking model, whether this is an add-on to your full-time income, or whether you're doing this as your primary income, we're going to do it professionally. If we're going to do this, let's do this. Be a professional, we are going to follow up with all of our leads. If our prospect says, "I'm going to think about it."

We will always follow up. It's on them to give us that definite answer.

JC:

That's the same in any business interaction. It's a yes or a no, or it's a maybe. Maybes will drive you nuts. It's easier just to say no.

CP:

The challenge for most people is they know these people personally, and they don't want to come across as being pushy to their friend. But you're addressing your friend with a business model, so you need to compartmentalise with which character are you. Are you in the friend character? Or, are you in the business character?

And yes, you've got the one that's both, but when you're playing both roles, you need to be able to cross over in both steps, switch on, switch off. This is weird. I guarantee you if you get a complete stranger that walks into your work and you're offering goods or service and they say, "Well, let me go and think about it." You don't care whether they come back or not because you're getting paid for your time. But if it was a performance-based role where you only get paid if you perform, I guarantee you'll ask them, "What is it that you need to think about?" Or, "what are you unclear about with this item, with this purchase, with this process, with the service?"

You're going to dig until you get a definite yes or no. At the end of the day, it's all about numbers. We've mentioned that several times – it's just numbers but you want a yes or no. For me, it doesn't matter if they become so uncomfortable that they become a no because that's all on them – it's got nothing to do with me.

I've had customers that say, "oh, that was really uncomfortable." That was because they didn't give me a yes or a no. You give me the no, and the conversations pretty much done. You give me, I'm going to think about it, then I want to know what you're thinking about. Remember, if we go all the way back to the list, the more information we have, the better we can contact, the better we can follow up with. All the information that we've gathered at the earliest stages of this process, of these steps that we're going through, is so that we can do a better job. I do have a second part, but I know you like to ask questions, so I will resist till you ask.

JC:

It's interesting because this brings up the issues around sales and selling and getting the money and asking for the order, closing the

deal, and all that stuff; it's an emotionally charged topic. I think you hit the nail on the head there – people are dancing around, and if they give you a straight yes or no, then its done. Integrity also springs to mind, because you can go two ways. You can either actually ask genuinely, "How do you feel about that? What're your thoughts on it? What did you like or did not like?" Or you can basically ignore them, assume the sale and don't give them the option. The nice way of teaching it is that you're genuinely asking the person for their feedback and you're not just saying, "Right, sign here."

There are books on sales courses – 101 sales course – that say the best way is to ask, "do you want it or not?" This gave the person a chance to say no, or they reply "send me something," or "I need to speak to my wife – let me go and do some research on these things." Generally, I think some people do need to think about it. I think the introverts in the world do need time to compute and calculate. Again, that's why you need to follow up.

CP:

Exactly. If you now feel comfortable doing what I'm saying to do, and you want to allow people a way to think about it, that's fine. However, now that you brought that up, I would always encourage asking, "how about I give you a call in three days' time?" They're still in your funnel. Another thing is, like you said, "do you want it or not?" So, let's formulate a different clause. "Listen, I want you to have all the information that you need to make an informed decision because this is for your benefit. I get that this might not be for you, or the distributor side might not be for you, or whatever, you're not interested, so just let me know if you're not interested because I don't want you to feel like I'm being the pushy salesperson." Bring it on, let's talk about the white elephant in the room, so to speak." In their mind, they might be thinking, "Oh, I wish Chris wasn't being that salesperson. I can't believe he's doing this type of work, blah, blah, blah."

Bring it to their attention: "Look, I don't want to be that pushy salesperson that you may already be thinking I am. What I want you to do is make sure that you've got all the information so you can say yes or no but remember, you can say no. I just want to know where you're at with it."

This is my wording and process. However, find a way that you can address the fact and bring it to the table: "I don't want to be the pushy salesperson. What I do want is for you to have all the information that you can say yes or no. Let me give you a couple of days. I'm going to call you back and we'll decide what's happening. Either you are wanting to move forward or you're not." You've stipulated that there's going to be a follow up call. On that call, it's going to be the yes or no. It's just more detailed in a different way.

Let people have the time. Don't be pushy; have a more laid-back approach. Just realise it's expanding and extending your time frame. If you're okay with that, that's fine. Remember, it's okay to go slow just so that you can go faster later.

That all ties in with what you were saying earlier. You're sharing this information, not because you're getting paid to do the sales, but because you genuinely believe in your product, your service, the company, the project, the plan and the program. Remember the four Ps that we spoke about in the previous chapter: project, product, plan and program. You genuinely believe that one, two, three or all four of those are of value and benefit to them. You're telling them with their best interests in mind. That's the space that you want to always be in, with regards to building your business.

You're discussing something you're passionate about.

I actually found myself reading about a product to a client the other day and it was only after I'd walked away from the conversation, I realised that I'd done it, not because I was trying to sell the product. I was just saying, "this is a fabulous thing I use all the time. You should get into it because that problem you just mentioned could be fixed by this."

Refer back to the reason why you contacted them, if you have a wellness product or any product that ties in with your original contact message. You reference back to the reason why they said yes to seeing the information. Now you're at the stage after they've seen it, so reference back to the previous point where you said, "this program has the solution for the problem we first spoke about." You've got the loop kicking in. That's a really powerful way because then you're leading and also triggering why they said yes the first time, yes to the information. We just try to get them to say yes to acquiring the product or starting the plan.

Let's duplicate the full steps that you need to take, because this is where you build a business, this is where you find the team. This is about making sure that they're absolutely clear on what it is you're offering and why it's a benefit to them and ask them whether they want it or whether they don't. Getting a clear yes or no is the end result you're looking for.

If it gets to the point where they say no, I always say this: a no just means it's not the right timing. It doesn't matter when or where they say that in your process, it's just not the right timing for them to start, whatever your plan or product or business opportunity. Even after they've seen, they've got a bit of an idea of what you're talking about. When you do your 30 or 60 day follow up, you can go back with an update of a new product, service or development within the business, or a testimony about what the businesses or product achieved. Maybe there's an achievement within the networking industry, maybe you've achieved something. Maybe now you earn an extra $500 a week: "If you know anyone that wants to earn additional money every single week with a proven step by step system, let me know."

With a contact message, use an update and deflect. You update them with a testimony, success story or something along those lines, and then you deflect. The deflection is that you're telling them about the story, but not pitching to them — you're pitching to who they know. You need to see this testimony; she lost X amount of weight, or she's achieved that sort of skin. She's earning an extra $500 a week. Do you know anyone? As soon as they read or hear that, they'll think, "oh, I'm not getting pitched, they're asking me if I know anyone." So, the barrier goes down.

Then you stay it with: "do you know anyone who would want these results?" And you wouldn't just say, 'these results.' You would be very definitive of what you're stating, like bullet points: "do you know anyone that wants an extra $500 a week?" "Do you know anyone that would find benefit in having an extra $500 a week? Do you know anyone who would like to lose 5lbs, 10lbs in weight and have better health?

You can repeat that process until that one person eventually says yes, because eventually the timing will be right.

You've exposed them to so many pieces of information, that you've done a number of things.

You've shown your consistency — this wasn't just a fad for you — you've actually stuck it out and you're still building it, whether its 12 months or 24 months down the line.

Secondly, you've continually updated them about developments and it shows growth in the company and it shows that other people are getting whatever results that you're speaking about.

It also does a number of other things but basically, it makes you more approachable for when they are open to it. It does take people usually about four or five "no's" before they're ready to say "yes". That's a statistical sales stat, which is why we see the same adverts so many times on TV. We need to be exposed to the same pieces of information multiple times to convince us to then go and buy it. That's the same on the radio; we hear it multiple times so that we are hearing it and absorbing it and say, "you know what, I'm going to get it. Now it's the right time." Maybe you've seen something on the TV and said, "ah, no, I don't have enough money. It's not the right time." For that holiday or that item or whatever.

Maybe you got a Christmas bonus, or you were doing double shifts, or you took on extra shifts. Someone went on holiday and got extra money and it's like," now I'm going to get it." The timing is right, because you have the money or you have the time or your schedule's opened up in a way that allows you to do whatever it is.

We come across that all the time. I don't have the time to go the dentist this week, but I'll go to the dentist in three weeks' time. That's a timing issue. I don't have the money, it's a money issue. Sometimes there's value issues that come in as well, where they don't see the value in it, so they keep saying no, because they don't understand.

If you're doing these 30 to 60 day follow ups, you're giving them more education every 30 to 60 days on what's happening. Eventually, they're either going to say yes, they're going to ask for more information, or they're going to want more specific details. Or, they're going to tell you, "will you please, please stop messaging me about this." At this point, there are two things you can do. You either comply, no problem, and they come completely off your list. Or you can but ask for more understanding – "why are you saying no? Why don't you see that this is solving problem X, and this is the solution to your problem? This is why I've been sharing this with you. I've got a genuine vested interest in your well-being and your health, and you having a better life, a better lifestyle. Why do you keep telling me no, when I have something that's the solution?"

That's going to put them on the spot, and it's going to make them face the shit. The reason they'll say no, might be a lack of self-worth or a lack of self-value. You've brought them the key to their problem, whether that may be weight loss, skin conditioning, personal development, assets, or a business that generates income, whatever your company's offering; it's the solution to the problem. If you have a solution, and they're still saying, no, you've got to ask them, "why are you saying no to the solution?"

As a friend or someone who has a genuine interest in their well-being and their life, challenge them on it. Why are you punishing yourself? Why do you continue to stay in pain, discomfort, unhappiness, when I have a way to change that? It may not be the one and only way, but I have a way. I'm your friend and I'm your colleague — I want to help you in this. I've done X, this person's done X, we're all doing X together. Why don't you want to be part of that? Come from a place of compassion, a place of empathy, a place of community of nurturing, of nourishing, of wanting the best for them.

So those are two ways of responding. You either say okay, or you come from the space of caring for another person. That's up to you.

That's your choice, whether you take it that far. You might be a person that doesn't like confrontation, in which case you're not going to challenging anyone. But that's what you can do if they tell you that they no longer want to hear about this.

Another option is, instead of waiting 60 days, wait four months or maybe six months before you do it again. You want to be surrounded by the type of people that are like you and the people you aspire to be, so you're constantly putting your hand out. If they're always saying, no, eventually they may no longer be part of your circle, should you choose to let that relationship go. That's what happened with me. I've been so driven with my ambition and within my career and personal development, professional development, that I've moved on from many groups of friends.

It's not an easy choice to make, and it's not an easy path to take, but there are many sayings about this, you are like the five people you spend the most time with. Therefore, are they people you aspire to be, or are they people you would rather not end up like? If you're the smartest person in the room, if you are the wealthiest person in the room, you're in the wrong room. They are utilising what you have, on an energetical vibrational, personal development, professional development, or aura level, and you forgot to do it for yourself.

JC:

Sometimes someone who you're trying to help to your life raft will capsize your life raft if you're not careful. What I think is interesting is I am an example of someone who was approached on many occasions before I finally said, "okay, let me have a look at this." Then, next I said, "yes." Then it made me six figures.

The other thing that crossed my mind was the lovely situation to be in six months down the line, when someone is enjoying the benefits and has seen massive shifts and is thanking you for introducing them to it. It's very humbling, but it's a great feeling to see somebody thrive because they said, "yes."

CP:

That's why, in the network marketing industry, you get this real close, tight knit family feeling with your team. You're genuinely helping each other, and it can be an emotional roller coaster, but it can be gloriously rewarding. You're a member, depending on what system that the program runs on.

JC:

It's nice to be in a business environment where everybody genuinely wants you to be successful, because, frankly, you're making them successful as well. It's actually in everyone's best interest. Let's jump to part two that you had mentioned.

CP:

It's not so much part two, but it's a way of dealing with the person who sees the presentation and says, "Oh, no, no, no, this is not for me. I'm a complete, no."

So we don't just let those people go, let's dig a little bit. You've pitched your contact, the contact was successful because it got a yes so whatever you said resonated with them. You're now showing them the presentation, video, PDF, whatever it is, and now they've come back and they're a no.

The response to that is, "oh, really? What was it that you expected to see that you didn't?"

They're expecting to see something, based on your contact. Your bait was hooked, but the information wasn't what they expected to see, so you want to find out why. "What was it you expected to see that you didn't?" You're going to find out exactly what it was that they wanted. Then you can redirect them: "oh, did you not see it at this point of the presentation? Did you not see it at this point of the video?"

Then, because you know what it is, you don't need to have them re-watch it. You've got the knowledge of that section in the presentation, so you work it in a way that will show them what they were waiting to see but somehow missed.

Now you know what it was they were looking for, you can home in on that one piece of information, that one element they were hoping to see. "What was it that you expected to see that you didn't?" "Well, I thought XYZ was going to happen because you said this." "Oh, well, that was actually the best part of the presentation." And then you would explain that section. Then you can choose, "would you like to see more information about that particular element?" If you can really box into this and then send them one or two pieces of short information with videos, where they can then see the information they were expecting to see.

If you're giving them what they expect, are they going to be more receptive? Are they going to be more positive when you follow up with them, once they've seen that?

You can choose to either explain on the spot and then go into back and forth Q&A, or you can send them the information and then schedule the BPI for afterwards. You can do this because you now know what they're interested in. They just need to see a specific part of your product, your project, your plan or program.

JC:

It's almost like we've moved closer down your funnel. If we use a golfing analogy, you're no longer taking your first shot; you're 20 foot... why am I using golf analogy? I don't like golf

CP:

You don't play it at all.

JC:

You're 20 foot…

CP:

You're on the green.

JC:

You're on the green and your 20-foot putt has now become a 12 foot or a 10 foot, because you're getting closer and closer to the hole.

CP:

As you get to the hole, the easier the shot. I don't know where that came from, I can't even play golf. You're moving them closer and closer to the goal, which is to get a yes or to get a no, but ultimately to get a yes. But you're moving them closer and closer to giving you an answer. Of course, an answer more favourable for them because you're solving a problem and more favourable for you because they're signing up for something. That's the other element when we see no one's a blanket no. Avoid thinking, "okay, I'm never going to speak to them again, damn." Don't expect such a strong reaction, such a strong no or negative response.

If they were closed off, they would have said no in the contact. So, there's something about your contact message that allowed them to say yes. If they say no to your contact message, when you follow up with them, try a different contact message. Go back to your upline, explain the communication process and get some correction and feedback. Then you can go and apply the feedback and corrections they've given you to get a better response or increase your ratio of yes's to no's.

JC:

Are you a fan of Role Playing, with your upline?

CP:

I never used to be. By the time I was comfortable doing a role play, I was so good at doing this that I didn't need to. But I do this with my team. Yes, it's cringe worthy and it doesn't feel natural, because you've never done it before. It was never natural to drive a car until you learned the order of how your hands and feet coordinate together to get the outcome of the car moving forward.

Definitely, it's something that is beneficial to do, with your contacting and your follow up. Make a list of all the objections you have heard or can think of to what you do or go on to Google and type in what are the most common objections for MLM or Multi-Level Marketing, or network marketing. Go and find them. Find all the objections; arm yourself with objection handling skills.

JC:

Scripts?

CP:

Yep, scripts, and be prepared for all those questions and objections so that you can say, "Great. I'm really happy you said that." In your head you're like, "I know exactly what I'm going to say here. Hit me with the pyramid scheme, hit me with the scam, hit me with whatever it is." Whatever they chose to. The more practised you can be on objections, the more practised you can be with Feel, Felt, Found, the smoother your follow up will be. It will be very impressive to your contacts, that you're able to deal with everything in a very relaxed, calm manner.

It's not about having an excuse for everything they say. If they're correct, they're correct. The majority of the time, they wont buy because they don't understand either the project, the product, the plan, or the program.

It all comes back to the four Ps within the presentation, which ideally your company presentation addresses. If you create a presentation, address them specifically.

Again, there's a process here. It's battle tested, it's proven, it works in the real world.

Your contact can be rubbish, your information can be rubbish, but if you can follow up, that's where the magic is.

As I've shared, the majority of my building has been through Facebook. I went into a network marketing coaching plan and went into the private group for it. Of course, the rule was: no pitching each other. This was because we were all in network marketing companies. However, if someone asked you what you do, that was the green light. Of course, when you're within a community, you connect and add people and such. I went and made some connections. When I stopped doing the coaching and came out of that community, I still had the contact, so straight away I was following up. I messaged someone about the company that I'm currently working with, and I can't remember how it went but basically, eventually, they got a free account.

Then I was speaking to a cross-lane affiliate within our company that I became friends with – you eventually get to know everyone, and as you're moving up the ranks people recognise you and such. This guy and I are quite friendly. Let's use names. Let's say Bob contacted John.

John's already the crossline affiliate. Bob is my free account that took forever to get registered. Bob started prospecting. Well, it seems that he started prospecting and John turn right to Bob and said, "You know, I'm already in on this." "When did you get an account and who did you get one with? Because I've been telling you about this for ages." Bob said, "I got in with Christopher Peacock." John said, "Are you kidding me?" And Bob's response was, "I've been telling you, about this." "Chris is a machine when it comes to following up – he just didn't give up."

The lesson there, is just don't give up. For John, that was actually the second person that happened to him. I ended up sponsoring someone else that was within his circles. It's not seen in any way unethical or immoral or bad blood or anything. He was just surprised that these contacts which were completely outside of Scotland – one being overseas – how I was able to do what I did. It all came down to follow up and how persistent I was.

It's not a great feeling to meet someone who you pitched to, maybe a year down the line, and it turns out they signed up with someone else, because you didn't follow up with them.

JC:

You didn't, but somebody else did.

CP:

You didn't continue to follow up, you didn't do the update deflect. Always revisit each contact within every 30 to 60 days. The reason for that is you don't want it to happen to you. If you're showing them your company offering, you're the person they're going to remember, you're the person they're going to get back to. The reason why they stuck with me was because there was no overall relationship.

It wasn't a friend. We were all contacts on social media that went into a similar community. Then it's in our hands. I'm persistent, ambitious and hungry. I followed up. Regardless of what they choose to do, it doesn't matter. At any point, they can get switched on and plugged in within my team's community for this project, for this company, that

I'm working with now. Fortune is always in the follow up. That's the key element of all these steps.

If you don't do this, you're going to struggle. It'll be hard work. That's the effort and pain. If you do it, it's battle tested, it's proven it works. It's quick, it's easier. Once you learn how to do it, it's just rinse and repeat. Straight forward.

These are life skills. This is not just for network marketing. We spoke in the contact section about FORMB: Family, Occupation, Recreation, Message, and Booking an Appointment. FOR: Family Occupation Recreation. That's communication skills; that's life skills. You can adapt that into any business you're doing, whether it's networking or not. You're building the life skills to build relationships to have good communication and have a little bit of a silver tongue, I think is the phrase, isn't it? It's the gift of the gab, to have the charm and charisma, where you've honed your skills and communication to get responses that you want.

Success goes to those who are determined and persistent. Its persistence and consistence that will build your business. Get into this every day. Meet the approaches, meet the follow ups and your business will grow, simple as that. If you don't, it won't.

Chapter 07 – Training

CP:

Today is step seven - focusing on training. Not to be confused with the step after, which is coaching. Coaching and training are different things.

The way that I look at it, is that training is company specific. It's knowing the orientation of your website, knowing the orientation of your back office, your dashboard. Where do I get this information? Where is the compensation plan stored in PDF format? Where are the special offers?

The training stage is about landing your company specific details. Maybe you've got video tutorials, PDF tutorials, or maybe you're with a newer company that doesn't have those things set up yet. You need to go in, fish about and find your way. Whether it's your upline directing you or whether you are just having a bit of a nosy, it's very important to take a time to know how you do your steps. Can you create an account for your customer, or your new distributor, or your affiliate? Can you then take them through a purchase? Can you explain the compensation plan? Can you break it down?

If we go back to the commitment, we spoke about learning and relearning. Listening and re-listening, learning and re-learning. Repetition is key. The repetition of how to sign someone up will eventually be memorized; you'll be able to do it without even seeing the visuals of the signup process. That'll be the same for the purchasing process, regardless of the product. And eventually, with repetition, repetition, repetition, you will know that inside and out, blindfolded.

The reason I'm connecting this back to step two, which is the commitment, is because you're committing your time. Part of the time commitment for your business is specifying an element of time, a period of time for your training.

If this was a job, you'd be taught this information by the staff trainer. Maybe your upline or your sponsor will do this with you, or maybe you've got PDF tutorials or video tutorials. It's about spending a little time to know your office – your online office. If you go into a new job, you need to be shown where the filing system is, where the invoice is going, where the deposits go, where stock goes, and where the stock forms are. It's just your logistics.

It's not something I spend a lot of time on because I like to make tutorials, especially with platforms where you can record your screen on video. You don't need to actually create a presentation – you just log in and record the screen. Where to go, how to find your referral link, how to sign people up, if there are backup orders, how you do those. You probably already have corporate specified ones. If you want to be the person that everyone looks up to, then you can go in and make your own. Making your own is also a way for you to concrete your own learning, because the quickest way to know what you're doing is to teach someone else what you've learned: Learn Do Teach. So, you've learnt it, you're doing it, now go and teach it – this will solidify everything. This chapter will probably be very quick because it's simply committing to getting to know what you are using, getting to know your platform, getting to know your compensation plan – the ins and outs of the logistics.

JC:

Can I take you back to the opening sentence there, about the difference between training and coaching? Coaching you're going to cover in the next chapter, but how do you see the difference between the two?

CP:

Training is what we do. Coaching is how we do it.

So, the training: you can only sign up a customer with screen shots, with the steps in front of you. If you've got a three or four step purchase process, they will always be the same three or four steps. However, the coaching side of it is more mindset, personal development. Coaching goes all the way back to, 'do you know why you're doing this, step one, the vision?'

Step 2 is, 'have you made a commitment to yourself and your time?' The personal development side of it, the mindset side of it, is what's going to be in the coaching. So, the training is what we're going to do; we'll get you a free account, we'll take you through setting that up, we'll get you a package, and we'll choose which one it is. The 'how' is, 'how did we get to that stage'? Well, we made a list. We qualified everyone. Then, we contacted them with a very specific contact message. We then presented them the information and followed up with them and made sure that they had all the information they need to have an answer of yes or no. Now, they've obviously said yes, because now you're at the step of going through our registration with them. So, through all of those steps and processes, the coaching is key. The coaching is keeping yourself as well as your team motivated, keeping them inspired, keeping them tied into a positive mindset. Are they studying? Are they watching and re-watching, listening and re-listening to industry specific items, or something that you've recommended? Are they following specific industry or motivational speakers? Coaching is all mindset. It's all about personal professional development.

The training is just very straight forward, almost analytical. If you've got four steps, how do you go through the four steps?

JC:

This is quite a lot! It was great that you took me through each step – go there, click that, do this. And we're using technology so we can share screens, so you can see where you're going. Or you can find the handouts or the video. In a job, you'd need to know what drawer the stapler is in, where the confidential waste goes, when the tea break is. You need to know all these things in a normal working environment. The difference with this is that it's on the screen. But, it's still the basics. Would you advocate that someone in a new network spends time familiarising themselves with the online systems?

CP:

Get familiar but it's not that it isn't a priority, don't allocate a lot of time to it because, it's not an income producing activity. This is the first time I've used this phrase. The key income producing activity is a registration with someone purchasing.

Your learning of the company plan does not put anyone through the steps to get registered. It's your learning, your teaching and your study. You use Learn Do Teach, even in these initial steps. The first few steps are the educational learning parts. Then we've got the doing part, and then we'll get to the teaching part. The last two steps, including this one, is the teaching element. The doing element is your contact lists, your presentation and your follow up. The learning element is learning while you're doing this, and then giving time to your commitment. Within your commitment, you've got your learning time – how much time you're allocating to learning.

Coming back to training, remember in a previous chapter I said if you're travelling on public transport, it's dead time. So that's an excellent time to review tutorials. It's an excellent time either to listen to an audiobook, a tutorial, or watching either of the two. Utilise your time as much as possible.

Now here's a key – it's regularly repeated that the biggest element of your business should be prospecting. That's when you're going out and contacting cold contacts, warm contacts, hot contacts. And that you want that activity balance to be about 80%. So, it's not even a balance – you want about 80% to be the active business building side of the prospecting. You can build this business without having any knowledge of your product or your compensation plan or how to set up, because that's what your upline is there for. So remember, it's 'invitation > presentation > three way validation.

You don't need to know the how. You just need to know that you can reference someone to take them through it. Especially with new people, it's very much learn as you go.

The analogy is you've got a good driver and a bad driver. They both drive the car, but their mindset is whether they drive well, or they don't drive well. I think that's a great analogy for training and coaching. In the training, both people are driving the car because technically they know how.

JC:

They passed the test.

CP:

Yeah, exactly, the coaching side is the mindset. It's about, are they a calm confident driver? Erratic and unsafe. Road rage ready to erupt.

JC:

It's triggered a memory again. I remember someone in my downline would ask, "How many points of volume is this product worth?" or, "how much profit do I get on the sale of every one of these?" I would answer, "I have no idea. I couldn't tell you, because I don't care about that. I care about hitting that next rank; I care about qualifying for this target; I want the free trip to LA," or wherever it was. So, I'm focusing on activity – four days out of five should be approaching and contacting. One day I'll spend training, and I'll work out how many volume points I get. But as far as the compensation plan goes, I have no idea. I don't care at all; all I'm interested in is getting it done. That's how I was taught.

CP:

Okay, so just remember that the training element is a small percent, maybe 5-10% of your time. 80% of the time should be prospecting.

10% you're filling in with motivational stuff or mindset stuff. So again, you've got 80% prospecting and 20% admin, and team admin, inventory, some study and learning. The balance is tipped very much into the activity of building the business without needing to know how someone gets 100 bv or gv or points or units, or whatever it is. The training element is essential because your upline doesn't want to have to always sign up your people for you. That is something that you will learn and then move into doing on your own. What'll eventually happen is, when you're doing the business partner introduction calls, they'll get shorter and shorter because you're capable of doing more and more. Consequently, your upline is needed less and then fulfils the business partner introduction side. This is where you've found a contact or prospect, but your upline is the expert, so your upline borrows the trust and credibility and influence from your relationship with that contact. In return, you get to borrow the expertise of your upline, so that your contact sees you as connected to that.

What will end up happening in your beginning days, is that once your upline has done q&a, they will then support you registering them on the spot, ideally, at least a free account if not then moving into products or a package of some sort. Then, as you progress, your upline will only be doing the q&a. They'll jump off as soon as q&a is finished, then you'll take over and sign them up, register them, get the pack done, because you know how to do it all. That saves their time and your time as well.

JC:

And at the same time, you'll be teaching your guys how to do the same things.

CP:

It's the duplication principle in action.

JC:

Do think this is a topic that people struggle with? I always thought you're quite fortunate in a network marketing business, because you're given a lot of support, you're getting a lot of training, a lot of the heavy lifting has already been done for you. You're essentially being handed a franchise – a system that works. It's whether or not you'll work it, you know, but all the steps, it's all there.

CP:

Yeah, the main problem is people spend too much time on it.

JC:

They spend too much time on it. And what is it? It's not an income producing activity. So, the mindset kicks in again – people procrastinate because the contacting element is the challenging part. Sitting down watching or reading tutorials is very easy. I can play about in my back office or learn about the comp plan today. Great – how many people did you contact? Err...none. Okay, so today your business was closed...? We had a staff training day!

CP:

The main problem is giving it too much time. It's also a bit of a cop out from doing the activity. Also, some people come from a space of being a perfectionist. They get caught in the trap of wanting to be the expert. They want to be the source of the information – the source of all the knowledge – so that they can shine. Before getting into the networking world, I was stuck in being the expert. My education and knowledge, and the clients I was working on was mind-blowing. I was used to knowing my information inside and out. Then, coming into the network world where different companies, different comp plans, different products, product knowledge, compensation plan, company knowledge and vision. I was caught up on wanting to be able to speak with all the knowledge that I have on this company.

But that way, you're not being duplicatable. If you're sitting there doing it all and the person you're speaking to is an average Joe Bloggs, who, regardless of intelligence level or skill level, does it show them that this is an easy business to start? Or are you actually putting them off by showcasing just how much you know? It's better to plead dumb and leverage your upline purely to show the step by step system. I still do three-way calls with my upline and they are done in 15-20 minutes, because it all depends on the person and how many questions they have. He will actually state, 'this is really just a formality to show you the system here. Chris is more than capable of going through all of these questions with you and getting you set up. But if you've got anything else, I'm happy to answer; if not, Chris will take over it was a pleasure to meet you and I look forward to working with you'.

It just depends on how many questions there are. My upline stays until all the questions are addressed. I don't answer anything. But as soon as they say, "I'm ready to go," he jumps off and I jump in and take over. It's time efficient for him. It's showing the duplication model. And the point in telling this story is that again, you don't need to know everything or be the source. It's actually better if you're not the source of information, because it shows this is easy to do, or at least it's simple. It's not an easy business; it's not a get rich quick scheme or a get rich overnight plan. But it is a simple business model and plan! A business of copy and pasting what has been shown to work previously.

JC

Yes.

CP:

The difficulty people face is spending too much time on it and getting caught up on thinking they need to know it all before they speak to anyone.

JC:

Or trying to reinvent the wheel, or trying do it their way, or making it more complex than it needs to be. Talking from experience here.

CP:

Just follow the system that works. KISS. Okay?

The training is a very easy topic for us and there's not a lot to get into. And we've covered more than enough around the training. And this chapter's small because it's a small part of what you're doing. You'll notice that the size of the chapters reflects how much time you should be putting into it.

Chapter 08 – Coaching

CP:

The final step of my 8 step system is the coaching and it's all about the mindset of how. We used the analogy of the bad driver and the good driver before. Both of them are driving so both of them have done their training, but the reality of whether they have a good trip or not is all based on their mindset. Did they wake up cranky? did they have an argument with their partner in the morning? Have they set off in a bad mood, and it's just a bad day all day long? They drove badly, people cut them off, there were horns blaring. This is compared to the nice relaxed person that woke and did a meditation, floats out of the door to their car and enjoys a very leisurely journey listening to nice music and lets people in when they give way. Nobody's getting cut up because they've given way. Their mindset is very much clear and calm. That is all down to coaching and mindset, and that is very much the case in this industry as well.

We have our highs and lows, just as we do in our sales throughout the season in the networking year. You also will have your highs and lows with your emotional states because a lot of people come in with the expectation that 'I love this so everybody's going to love it as well – everybody I speak to is going to say yes!' If that expectation isn't squashed by the coach, sponsor or upline, and put into a more realistic position, they will have a very turbulent career and experience in network marketing and may not make it past that first year. The mindset is key to keep you balanced. You'll always have the peaks and troughs; you always have the highs and the lows, but it's better to have gentle ups and downs rather than the extremes. We want to bring that range closer to the middle.

The coaching centres around, how are you setting your mindset? What are you doing to keep your mindset positive? If you're facing challenges, how do you change your state? Tony Robbins is a massive advocate of changing your state. And it can be done very easily and quickly. You can do breathing exercises; you can do press ups until can't do any more. You can run up and down the stairs, do 10 jumping jacks, burpees if you're feeling more energetic. However, changing your state can be done very easily and quickly on a physiological level, meaning movement integrating your body. And the physiological changes in your state has an emotional reaction. It's about arming ourselves so that we can combat ourselves.

JC:

I've been in network marketing three times and I forgot just how much of an inner game it is. In my opinion, it's you versus you. It's

all down to you. That's why I think there's such a strong connection between network marketing MLM and personal development. You really need that self-development component to be your safety net and your life jacket and your confidence boost. You need it because you're going to get rejection; you are going to get people who just don't get it; you are going to get criticism.

I remember running a business opportunity meeting, a BOM. I invited a whole bunch of people to a local pub where I was going to give a presentation. A woman came up to us at the end and just slated... not our particular product, but that type of product. Apparently, it had ruined her health. I wasn't really buying her story, but I could see she was standing there publicly causing a problem for us and killing the atmosphere. I could respect that she'd had an experience in her life, but I came away from that and I wished it hadn't happened. That really spoiled it for everybody. So, it's important to be able to bounce back from challenges. There are good days and bad days – you need to get back on the horse.

CP:

In the beginning, I had extreme highs and lows. Someone came in and bought a package or bought the pack – like the stereotypical pack that everyone starts with regardless of whether they're a customer or not – and I was up! I was like, "yes I just got a new sale!"

Then, maybe there were a couple of yes's. When you're on a roll, you're on a high. But then the no would come in, because it's a numbers game. There's always going to be a no, but the worst ones were the no's that I thought were going to be yes's. That would tank me, and I would be down. I would be up and down and it was tiring to say the least.

My upline at the time tried to keep me on an even keel and encouraged me to have more harmony and flow. I don't like to say balance because balance is just like straight line. A flat line means you're dead. We want some fluctuation on these things. My upline had a challenge with me, being up and down. That was the same thing over and over again, until I got a bit more control over it.

It's not about being in control. It's about having the tools that arm yourself on how to combat your own negativity and things that come up. You know yourself better than anyone else and you are more critical of yourself than anyone else is. You know when you're going to trip up because you're the one tripping yourself up. If you know what your weaknesses are or where you typically will fall, it's very easy to then find a tool or a key that can help prevent it. You can use them to be proactive or reactive, so when you're down you're only down for a shorter period of time, before you come back up to a normal state. Make sure have these tools to hand, whether its compilation, motivational speakers, meditation, exercise or downtime and relaxation.

If you don't have a family, and you are a single person, there is something else to consider. This is a home-based business. You're no longer around people and you're doing a lot of screen time, unless you get to go to local events. The inner game is even more important for those of us who are going to work online more.

The mindset is very much key, which is where all your coaching will come into it. Your sponsor can direct you to a range of different network marketing industry specific stuff, or motivational speakers who may or may not have been in the industry.

Also, if you're not working on your mindset and your inner game, then you're not training yourself to receive more. If you're not trained to receive more than what you're used to receiving, how can your income grow? You're not feeling worthy enough to receive an increase in your income because you've been getting 20 grand or 30 grand for however many years in your day job or self-employed job. In a self-employed position, you're the boss. You're the accountant. You're the receptionist. You're the bookkeeper. You're the janitor. You are the coach. You are the person who is actively working. You represent every element of your business.

You come from that space where you're doing everything and you're receiving the income you're receiving. Over the years, you've got into a rhythm of being at that level. Yet, the only way to raise your financial thermostat, to be able to turn it up and raise your financial blueprint to higher income level, is if you start to work on your personal development. This includes your self-worth, your self-value, your self-belief. You believe you can achieve more and that you are worthy of receiving more.

If you don't work on that stuff, you trip yourself up because those subconscious programmes are already preset from when you were growing up as a child. Your parents, grandparents, teachers, friends, experiences that you've had in previous businesses, or when you've observed family, friends, family members going into business, going bankrupt, losing money, getting scammed, being conned. It's essentially whatever your experiences are around money, which is again all personal development stuff.

I spoke to a couple of people who were in Amway in its heyday. One of the regular comments that I heard was that the personal development plan was amazing. It was almost like a train or a conveyor belt of books that you worked your way through – a conveyor belt of personal development. If you've not got recommendations, look them up. Some of the network marketing books are very quick reads and they have some great golden nuggets of information.

JC:

An awful lot of the personal development household names were originally network marketers. The whole seminar model to this day comes from the network marketing industry.

CP:

I think it's Robert Kiyosaki that says there's two or three ways to get rich and it's all around systems.

Straight away we've got the network marketing system where you're leveraging the efforts of many and leveraging your time, which is similar to a franchise system. However, it will cost you anywhere from quarter of a million to get into a good franchise. The network marketer model doesn't. The third system that will make you wealthy is to develop a system yourself, but will probably take the longest because, one, you need to create it; two, it really needs to be successful; and three you need to be able to get it out there so it becomes viral and then it becomes used, and so it becomes self-perpetuating. So, there are a few ways and Robert Kiyosaki says that in his Cashflow Quadrant book.

Network Marketing is the simplest of those three options. It's also the cheapest because with most companies, you can get started from as low as 50 bucks. With the majority of companies, some of them may be a little bit higher, say 100 - 500 for decent packs. However, in a stereotypical traditional business, you're looking at anywhere between 10 to 20 grand to get started.

The coaching is key. Accountability is also part of the coaching – making sure that you have an accountability partner. Who do you have as your accountability partner, a peer, someone that you're running with? Or is your accountability partner your coach or sponsor?

Make yourself accountable. Make sure that you're having regular contact with your coach and make it valuable. It's not just a chit chat or a catch up. Take inventory – what have we done this week or what did you do? Take inventory of your action and activity. That's also accountability. You said yesterday that you're going to contact five people – did you contact five? What did you do? What was the result? What happened from it? The ones that didn't work, why? Why do you think it didn't work?

With coaching your team, you suggest the correction and then you encourage them to go and do the corrections. You give feedback, get feedback, share the correction and then have them go out and do that correction. Then, the next time you follow up and have another accountability session, ask how it went. If those messages weren't working, do some role play. Ask them to contact you.

Soon, you start to adapt, and it becomes a very individualised coaching session for the person. It's not just copy and paste; you're responding to the level of success based on usability of knowledge.

If you don't know what's going wrong for them, then go to your upline and say, "Look I'm working with so and so. They're doing everything that I'm telling them to do but are still struggling. Can you have a call with them and see if I'm missing something, or can the three of us do a call where I am listening in on the conversation?" Then you're getting upline coaching on your coaching, so it's an ongoing process. But the coaching is something that happens from step one and all the way through. It can be anything that is stopping people from moving forward with their mindset – have they got a clear goal, vision, purpose, need? What's their why? What is their real core need?

I've worked with people where their financial need was so strong because they needed to pay for medical bills for their Dad. The dad was moving from one country to another because of the availability of medical care, but also the cost. That money was being sent back home. They needed to make money because they needed medical care for the father. Cause and effect. So, what's your need?

Is there a gap in someone's ability or success because they didn't clearly identify step one – the vision and everything that comes out on step one? Have they committed themselves and are they achieving what they set themselves to achieve, and do they need to re-evaluate their commitment? Is it too much for them at the moment? Is it too little? Are they listening and re listening to coaching, to mindset, to tutorials? Do they understand what they're doing?

Step three – are they being overly positive when scoring people? Are they scoring them too high so now they're actually contacting people with the wrong timing, with the wrong qualification? Is it the wrong contact message? Do they have enough information? Family occupation recreation? Do they know enough FORMB before they ever message or book the appointment? Once they've done the contact, are they getting eyes on the information? If they're not getting eyes on the information, then it's not the information – it's got to be how they're doing the contact.

If they aren't getting eyes on the information and they're still getting a 'no', then it's going to come down to the follow up or the timing. So again, we're back to the list and the qualification of when we're doing the contacting. There are a number of moving parts. It's almost like chess, though not as complicated as chess. There are a number of moving pieces and you need to become bit of a detective to find those. Where are they going wrong? Where's the kink in the chain? Where's the weak link? Find that and then make amendments and make adjustments to counteract what's going on. Do whatever it takes to shift that. Do they need different motivations? Do they need different mindset tools or learning? Do we need to swap to a different speaker, if they're listening to motivational people? Do they need to bring in something completely new? Do you need to get them to contact differently get them to step out of their comfort zone? Are they texting people when they should be calling them? Are they avoiding speaking to the person that's next to them in the bus for 45 minutes while they go to work? Every moment of your life, there is an opportunity to create a conversation and step out your comfort zone.

If you are stuck at home, working on screen, not going to any local events, not building your team fast enough, why aren't you going to local events? Why aren't you mixing it up by doing other things? What's not working?

The other element of this, especially when you're taking this forward to your team, or to your newest team member, your new person that's signed up, is: are they coachable? Are they doing what you set them to do? And if they're not, when do you cut ties? You want to give your time and energy to people that are doing what has been stipulated. Someone's always making excuses.

Maybe it isn't the right time for them. Why are they not doing it? There's a possibility they don't see the value in giving their business the time that they've got. It's the kids? They're tired after work. Whatever the reason may have been the reason they took the opportunity in the first place. So sometimes it's a reminder of why they got started. Tough love. I have quite a strong, direct personality. My tough love sometimes comes out too easily. But always work with them. Try your best to work with your personality. If they're quite a soft person, try not to be the dictator with them, but try not to be mum and dad.

There's a lot that can come into this coaching chapter. There are so many layers, so many different levels, so many avenues. But it all comes back to being positive, being persistent and consistent in your activity. If you're not doing activity, not taking action, you don't feel like it. You can't be bothered. You're not using the tools know you have, to change your own state. That's going to be particularly difficult and relevant for those people that are working less with an upline, or don't have one, or don't have access to a local team. If they can't plug in locally, and only on the big screen, it's all down to them to create the local team, affiliation and community.

It's going to be hard and will take time. Remember that family and friends are the most critical and have fewer filters, than lukewarm contacts at work or someone on social media and never met.

The world is very small now. You can have a completely global network very quickly from Hawaii all the way to New Zealand. Cover all the time zones.

I'm always on UK time but my morning was for UK, Europe, Australia and New Zealand. And then as I moved into the afternoon, it was UK, Europe and the east coast of North America. And as it moved into my early evening, the rest of North America would wake up, and then I'm getting to the morning for Australia, New Zealand, again in Asia. The middle of Europe obviously hits in most of those time zones as well. I used to joke and look at my schedule not as an hourly schedule but as a time zone schedule. I started to work on time zones; it's an interesting way to look at it. It changes your mindset.

JC:

I like that a lot. I think that would be a useful thing to encourage your team to do in your network, if you want to operate in other countries.

CP:

Yeah, that's a key way that I make money while I sleep. I've got a team on the other side of the world that is awake while I'm sleeping. If you want to make money while you sleep, then build across as many time zones as possible.

JC:

Okay, may I comment a couple things you said?

CP:

Of course you can.

JC:

I like the analogy that, every now and again, it pays to stop and look at your business process and the results you're generating. You've got eight steps here, sort of like the gas engineer comes out and is looking for the leak. Where is it? How far along the pipe before we smell gas? Once you find that block in the pipeline, you now know it worked up to that point and there's where we dropped the ball. Maybe I need some coaching from my upline on that particular point, and then we will really nail that one. We all have strengths and weaknesses.

One thing that triggered in my head was: when you've got a team, that it's very easy to want success for your team member more than they do. You're desperately trying to give them the leg up and you're trying to support them and motivate them to keep going. The truth is sometimes you need it for them more than they need it for them. And that can be an energy drain.

CP:

It's funny that you mentioned that. That's a trait that to this day, I still have a lot of challenge around. Because I want that success. I've got so much hunger, drive and ambition – my hunger, drive and ambition are so high that I can give plenty to other people. It's above and beyond where they're at. And I want them to have the benefits that I am experiencing, the success that I'm having, so badly for the people that I work with that I need to rein myself in on the expectations or their action because they can only go as fast as they can go. That means their mindset might not be ready, the skill level might not be there yet., their time is limited. They're not working the same number of hours in this industry as I am, because I've already done that. They're on day one; I'm several days in. I've already got a big head start and what we need to do is always remind ourselves, we're well ahead of the person that just came in. And when you're well ahead, there's only so far you can reach back to put your hand out for them to take it. They may be so far back that it's not your hand they're taking. It's the one or two or three people in between you that they have taken.

That analogy doesn't necessarily mean that you're not working with them directly. It's just about reminding yourself of when you started. What was your situation when you started, compared to theirs? Are they in a tougher place with less time? If so, they'll go slower. Are they as hungry as you were? Did your hunger grow like theirs will once they see results? Remember they've just started so they haven't seen results yet.

I've had to accept that some people are not meant for this business at the time. They may come back in two or three years' time and blow it out of the water. For a lot of people, you lead them to the water, but it's up to them to drink. That's the best we can do.

In my early days, I did try the hot poker thing – prompt them, remind them. I thought I was motivating people and encouraging them and keeping them in the loop. But it was very tiring and draining for me because if I compared what I was doing to them, my sponsor never needed to do that to me, because I was always asking them, can I get a call? I'm stuck. I realised that the people that I was trying to encourage... none of them were asking for it.

So, instead of being on and off, zero or 100, hot and cold, I needed to find the grey in between the black and the white. That's something that I've been working on. I decided that if they weren't asking for it, communication stops, and let's see if they notice.

A lot of people didn't respond. And that's okay – maybe they are just consumers or users of your product, services or goods, whatever it is. And maybe they're just investors. Maybe they're just not ready yet. Like I said, the timings not right. They thought they were ready.

They're not doing anything. Again, that goes back to step one – did they do step one? Did they have their vision? The why, the purpose, the need? Everybody wants to have a better life for their kids.

Everyone wants to provide more for the family. They say it, but are they really willing to do what it takes? Are they willing to get paid a little for doing a lot now, so that in the future, they can get paid a lot for doing a little? We've said this already in previous chapters. It's a classic Les Brown line.

JC:

The best judge of someone is not what they say but what they do.

CP:

Like the saying, 'being a man of your word', which obviously in this day and age is not PC. Be a person of your word. Thinking of those, do your words match your actions? A lot of people are all talk, all wind, but no gumption. Is that because they're worn out and tired? They've already been worn down by the system. Is there something you can do to get that spark back? Is there a way for you to drop those breadcrumbs that they start to follow and stay plugged in at that minimum amount until that time is right? Only you will know. And it's going to be a learning curve for you.

To cut people off, to reduce the energy you give them, might be down to how much energy you want to give people. Do you want to give a lot of energy to people that are doing a little? Or do you want to give a lot of energy to people that are taking action in their and your business?

JC:

Winston Churchill had a great phrase, along the lines of, 'success is staggering from one crushing disappointment to the next crushing disappointment without losing enthusiasm'. I love that. It's like, they ain't going to stop me – bring it on! Come and have a go if you're hard enough.

CP:

It's okay to have down moments and down days and accept those.

It's important to be compassionate with yourself and accepting of the highs and the lows. You'll know that because you're learning this, it's going to be challenging. You need to be okay with not being perfect from the beginning, and avoid comparing yourself to your sponsor who's going to have several years' experience on you, whether it's life experience, industry experience or company specific experience. Leverage that. The beauty of this industry is that you leverage the professional you're working with.

Go easy on yourself. It's going to be challenging. It's a simple system that is not easy. It's not a get rich quick scheme, or an overnight success plan. That is a false term. And you see that across social media all the time... so and so exploded into the industry, or onto the market and made a huge success. But how long have they been building the skills and developing and honing their craft? 10 years? 15 years? 20 years? I've also had challenges with, how quickly can I build? Can I grow quickly? Can I increase my income? I've had to reign in my extremely high expectations of myself – that ties in with my level of perfectionism as well.

So, take it from someone that knows. Manage your expectations correctly and wisely.

Follow the steps that we went through. If there's something not working, we allow you to go back to step one. This book is essentially something that you can review, review, review. It could be a monthly, quarterly, bi yearly review, that you do minimum every year. Every new year, it's the time for reflection. It's time for the vision for the coming year. We review what you've been doing, we review the steps, we review your process. What have you achieved from your vision board, score them off. Use it as a marker of achievement.

JC:

Celebrate every victory.

CP:

Yeah. Every victory. The smallest one – if you get someone that picks up the phone, celebrate the victory. They picked up the phone. Yeah, he saw your name on his phone and he did not ignore it.

JC:

They watched the video.

It's funny because you remind me again about, 'be the product'. We are the product. Use the product, carry the product, wear the product – whatever the product might be. I always remember meeting up with a network marketing powerhouse who you

probably know. I met her for coffee in a hotel in Glasgow. She ordered two cups of hot water, and then we carried on the conversation. A few minutes later the waitress delivered two cups of hot water, and into them she poured the product. Before I know it, I'm drinking one product and I'm eating one of her bars. I thought that was so slick.

I'm now eating the product. I'm quite enjoying it and thought that was great. People are going to ask, "what's that you're drinking?" or, "how does that work?" Wear the badge, carry the book, do as the company tells you to do, because these things work. The first network I was in gave us these huge day glow badges. We wore them everywhere and people did ask about them. I thought, oh my god this works, so I wore it religiously.

It's easy to do; it's also easy to not do. The components are simple, they're straightforward, they work, they're battle tested. They are proven – you will be trained on them. Don't make it overly complicated; get out of your own way. All the steps are outlined in this book in a sequential way.

CP:

Just know that you can always restart your business. No matter how many years you've been in this industry, you can always restart. It doesn't matter whether you have a bad month or a bad quarter or a bad year. You can start from scratch any time you want, as often as you need, until you hone and master your company as well as the skills for building it.

It's like a computer game. You can restart at any point. Just because you missed a bonus or you've skipped a level by accident, in this industry you can you just reset. If you're doing social media marketing, you can delete it all and start fresh. You can do that very easily. You can go back to the drawing board, go back to the beginning of the book and do it like you never did it before. Re-evaluate.

JC:

Re-evaluate your mistakes.

CP:

It's key to know that no matter what you do, no matter how good or how bad you think it is, as long as you're moving forward, you're doing something right. You can utilise any of the skills and tools that are in this book as well as speaking with your upline and refining what you're developing.

And should you need to restart the game, start the game with this book!

Attention Network Marketers!

Get Rid of Your Network Marketing Problems And Build Your Business Like You've Never Built It Before...

Are you ready to succeed in networking by following a PROVEN plan, build your business like you've never built it before, and learn from a veteran Network Marketer who replaced his full time income in 12 months?

If the answer is YES, I'd like to offer you VIP access to the "From Zero To Hero" Online Course, including:

1. 8 Step by step modules that show you exactly what to do and when
2. A duplicatable system that works every time
3. A complete Coaching process for your next new team member
4. VIP access to Christopher Peacock for one on one support
5. Confidence that comes from following a proven plan
6. The latest thinking in what's working now

Also Understand that When You ACT NOW, You Also Get...

➢ VIP membership in Christopher's Private Facebook Group

➢ A free copy of Christopher's e-book "From Zero To Hero"

Every day that goes by your confidence and willpower drops. <u>Let's reignite your passion!</u>

100% Guaranteed

If the "From Zero To Hero" Online Course doesn't show you exactly how to succeed in networking by following a PROVEN plan... if it doesn't take you by the hand, step-by-step, build your business like you've never built it before... or if it fails to help you learn from a veteran Network Marketer who replaced his full time income in 12 months, then understand that you will receive a full refund, No Questions Asked!

You get all this for only £97...

But when you buy now - as a special marketing test I want to help 20 Network Marketers succeed - **you get everything for only £47!**

<u>Click Here Now to get access</u>

To Your Success,

Christopher Peacock

P.S. - Every minute you wait to get "From Zero To Hero Online Course" is another minute lost. You already know what HASN'T worked. Don't go another day trying to figure it out. Instead take advantage of this breakthrough programme to quickly and easily succeed in networking by following a PROVEN plan and more!

http://bit.ly/infinitymastery

Printed in Great Britain
by Amazon